ISBN 978-1-331-86942-9
PIBN 10244598

1 MONTH OF
FREE
READING

at
www.ForgottenBooks.com

By purchasing this book you are eligible for one month membership to ForgottenBooks.com, giving you unlimited access to our entire collection of over 1,000,000 titles via our web site and mobile apps.

To claim your free month visit: www.forgottenbooks.com/free244598

English
Français
Deutsche
Italiano
Español
Português

www.forgottenbooks.com

Mythology Photography **Fiction**
Fishing Christianity **Art** Cooking
Essays Buddhism Freemasonry
Medicine **Biology** Music **Ancient
Egypt** Evolution Carpentry Physics
Dance Geology **Mathematics** Fitness
Shakespeare **Folklore** Yoga Marketing
Confidence Immortality Biographies
Poetry **Psychology** Witchcraft
Electronics Chemistry History **Law**
Accounting **Philosophy** Anthropology
Alchemy Drama Quantum Mechanics
Atheism Sexual Health **Ancient History**
Entrepreneurship Languages Sport
Paleontology Needlework Islam
Metaphysics Investment Archaeology
Parenting Statistics Criminology
Motivational

THE MODERN READER'S BIBLE

A SERIES OF WORKS FROM THE SACRED SCRIPTURES PRESENTED
IN MODERN LITERARY FORM

v 16

DANIEL

AND

THE MINOR PROPHETS

EDITED, WITH AN INTRODUCTION AND NOTES

BY

RICHARD G. MOULTON, M.A. (CAMB.), PH.D. (PENN.)
PROFESSOR OF LITERATURE IN ENGLISH IN THE
UNIVERSITY OF CHICAGO

New York

THE MACMILLAN COMPANY

LONDON: MACMILLAN & CO., LTD.

1897

Norwood Press
J. S. Cushing & Co. — Berwick & Smith
Norwood Mass. U.S.A.

INTRODUCTION

THE present volume of the Modern Reader's Bible has a special subject which involves some differences in the arrangement of the book. It contains not an author but a *corpus prophetarum:* the 'Minor Prophets,' with the addition of Daniel. Such an introduction as I have attempted to previous volumes seems unsuitable in this case; I have thought it more convenient to place at the commencement of the notes to each author what I have to offer in the way of general remarks. Considerations of space have further obliged me to reduce to a minimum the explanation of particular passages; in place of this I have usually given an analysis of each discourse or other division of prophecy. With this must be remembered, what is the principle of the whole series, that the arrangement of the text is itself of the nature of a commentary.

Another point of arrangement should be explained here. All that in the Bible follows the eighth chapter of *Zechariah* will be found in the present volume under the heading 'Anonymous.' Every reader will be aware that the authorship of the latter part of *Zechariah* is disputed. Had it, however, been merely a question of disputed authorship, as with *Isaiah,* I should have considered the matter outside the field of the present work. But the issue in the present case is something entirely within the scope of the Modern Reader's Bible — the question of the divisions of the sacred books. The facts seem to be these. The prophetic literature of the Old Testament was arranged under the names of the reputed authors, ending with the book of Zechariah (our *Zechariah* i–viii) ; following these were anonymous prophecies with *subject-titles*. The last of these subject-titles was 'My Messenger' (Malachi). How positively this was understood as a subject-title is illustrated by the fact that the Septuagint translates it as 'angel,' and the Targum ascribes the authorship of the book to Ezra. But in process of time 'Malachi' was read as a personal name, and thus the closing section of the prophetic roll seemed to follow the general form ; it was natural then that the intervening sections with their subject-titles should attach themselves to the preceding book of Zechariah. This account of the matter seems probable in itself, and is further confirmed by New Testament references. Four passages from the latter part of *Zechariah* are cited in the New Testament : three of them are cited without the name of any author, the fourth is ascribed by St. Matthew to Jeremiah.* Now if an anonymous prophecy is

---

* *Matthew* xxvii 9-10; compare *Zechariah* xi. 12-13. The other passages are *Zechariah* ix. 9 (in *Matthew* xxi 5 and *John* xii. 15); chapter xii 10 (in *John* xix 37 and perhaps *Revelation* i. 7); xiii 7 (in *Matthew* xxvi. 31 and *Mark* xiv. 27).

being quoted, it is natural for Jeremiah, the lengthiest of the prophetic writers, to give his name to the whole roll of prophecy, as David has given his name to the whole collection of psalms. If, however, the writing had appeared under the name of Zechariah, St. Matthew could not have ascribed it to Jeremiah without being guilty of misquotation. Under these circumstances, to have followed the Biblical headings in this edition would have been to pronounce on a question of authorship; the plan I have adopted leaves the question open. In any case, authorship is a matter of importance chiefly to the historian. But it would have been a real literary loss to be deprived of the subject-title 'My Messenger,' which gives such unity and suggestiveness to the final division of prophecy.

It is hardly necessary to bespeak attention for the scriptures included in this volume. They are 'minor' only in length: for the rest, it is doubtful if any collection of miscellaneous literature has ever brought together so many writers of such surpassing interest. They stretch over a period of time which, on one theory of dates, is as great as that which in English literature separates Wycliffe from Browning. Of the individual prophets, Amos was a herdsman and dresser of sycomore trees; Daniel a mage, and one of a triumvirate administering a world empire; Jonah was a missionary; Micah a plain countryman; Zephaniah of royal descent; the rest have died away from human record leaving only their works to speak for them. As we go through these prophetic writings we are introduced to Babylon, land of mystery, of dreams and interpreters, of mutations in a single moment from an emperor intoxicated with omnipotence to the dim consciousness of beast life, from a royal orgy to the writing upon the wall of doom. We see the Chaldean again as a world conqueror, taking the nations in his net and sacrificing only to his drag. In one prophetic book Nineveh appears as a vast city of three days' journey, swept through and through with an infectious thrill of penitence; another prophet gives us a realistic word picture of Nineveh in her careless gaiety, Nineveh smitten with bewildering destruction, Nineveh desolate and a thing of the past. Here it is that we view most clearly the picturesque corruption of northern Israel, where the sterner Hebrew strain was adulterated by the luxury and joyous imagination of Tyre. At one point we have a glimpse of border warfare and border hate. Elsewhere the prophecies deal with Judah, or with Israel in general. We see this Israel in the full strength of national hope, looking for a King of Peace who shall enter in lowly triumph, and garrison his land, with his people as the weapons of his war. We see the ebbing of these hopes, and the gradual withdrawing of the Divine Shepherd, until Israel is left a flock for the slaughter. Jerusalem is presented under the siege, yet with mighty hopes of repentance and deliverance. The exiles are seen as a scattered 'church' witnessing in the heart of the Babylonian 'world.' In

Introduction &-

Haggai and *Zechariah* we have the return from exile, and
the reweaving of the strands of national life in renewed
Temple service, a recovered prophecy, and a princedom
taking the place of the old kingship. And *Malachi* re-
fleets the dull period when the impulse of the exile has
been exhausted, and there is nothing but a weary looking
for a Messenger of God, who shall effect a rousing for
which native energy is no longer left.

The sacred thought embodied in these varied scriptures
is at once varied and the same. Hosea loves to dwell upon
God's yearning love, the love of the husband for the fallen
wife, of the father for his prodigal son. Amos takes his
stand for morals as against religion itself, when the two
have irreligiously clashed. Micah presents the true and
the false prophecy contending in the struggles of daily life.
But other themes grow together into the one prophetic
theme of judgment — the Hebrew counterpart of our modern providence. With Nahum it is a judgment upon the
foe, as a form of mercy to God's people ; Jonah comes as a
corrective, with the thought of Jehovah's mercy extending
outside his people to the sixscore thousand innocents of
Nineveh. The mystery of judgment which troubled the
wise men of Israel — the impunity of the wicked — appears
in *Habakkuk* magnified to the scale of nations : this prophet's problem is the sight of the Chaldean allowed to prosper
and punish wickedness less great than his own. Several
of the prophecies are filled with a 'Day of the Lord': the

judgment regularly appears as a visitation first upon Israel, to destroy the evil that is in it; then there is a purification and restoration, and finally a judgment between Israel and the nations; there is at the last an inauguration of a heaven, but it is a heaven upon earth.

The literary forms under which this thought is conveyed 'cover the whole range of prophecy; moreover, they involve certain minor peculiarities of structure which render specially important what the present edition endeavours to supply — the reflection of literary structure in the printed page. The simplest of all literary forms is the story: this is ideally represented in *Daniel* and *Jonah*. For prophecy a natural form is discourse: the sermons of the Minor Prophets seldom remain at the dead level of discourse, but flash into realistic pictures or dramatic dialogue. In *Amos* the most artificial rhetoric is sanctified for spiritual effects; he has a grasp of style which can draw in even the preface as an artistic interruption. In *Hosea* scattered outbursts of prophetic truth in conflict with everyday life have crystallised into brief epigrams. In several prophets we have the ' doom form,' which produces in speech the effect which music produces when it combines recitative and song. The emblem — which is in prophecy what the fable is in philosophy — is used to express stages of spiritual declension or of advancing doom. Elsewhere we have the apocalypse, or great ' unveiling,' — unveiling of the future in a philosophy of history, and unveiling of the unseen world with its angelic spectators of human affairs. And drama is exhibited by the Minor Prophets in various degrees of fulness: Micah moulds a single brief thought in dramatic form; Hosea dares to embody in monologue the varying moods of Deity; Joel and Habakkuk give us the full force of the 'rhapsody' which is the dramatisation of the spiritual.

I write from the standpoint of literature, not of theology, and I cannot refrain from insisting once more upon the injury done to our liberal education by its ignoring of Biblical literature. The Hebrews no less than the Greeks were our literary ancestors; to train ourselves in the productions of the one and not of the other means a distorted culture. Criticism can never be scientific that makes its inductions from a single field; and the literature it neglects is rich in forms of the first importance, both for their artistic interest and as vehicles of profound thought and powerful feeling. Nor can I understand those writers who seem to assume that in elaboration and finish of literary detail the Hebrew Scriptures are inferior to the productions of the Greeks. Comparisons of merit can never be more than personal judgments; but, speaking for myself as a student of world literature, I do not know to what I should turn for specimens of literary perfection rather than to the rhapsodies of Habakkuk and Joel. And if to another class of readers this last remark appears objectionable because of the sacredness of Scripture as Divine Revelation, I can only answer that it must be a strange theology which can see incompatibility between Divine inspiration and perfection of literary setting.

*
* *

The text is that of the Revised Version, the marginal alternatives being often adopted. For the use of it I express my obligations to the University Presses of Oxford and Cambridge. A Reference Table at the end connects the numbering of this volume with the chapters and verses of the Bible.

DANIEL

AND

THE MINOR PROPHETS

THE BOOK

OF

DANIEL

THE BOOK OF DANIEL

i

Daniel and the King's Meat

In the third year of the reign of Jehoiakim king of Judah
came Nebuchadnezzar king of Babylon unto Jerusalem,
and besieged it. And the Lord gave Jehoiakim king of
Judah into his hand, with part of the vessels of the house
of God; and he carried them into the land of Shinar to
the house of his god: and he brought the vessels into the
treasure house of his god. And the king spake unto
Ashpenaz the master of his eunuchs, that he should bring
in certain of the children of Israel, even of the seed royal
and of the nobles; youths in whom was no blemish, but
well favoured, and skilful in all wisdom, and cunning in
knowledge, and understanding science, and such as had
ability to stand in the king's palace; and that he should
teach them the learning and the tongue of the Chaldeans.
And the king appointed for them a daily portion of the
king's meat, and of the wine which he drank, and that
they should be nourished three years; that at the end
thereof they might stand before the king. Now among
these were, of the children of Judah, Daniel, Hananiah,
Mishael, and Azariah. And the prince of the eunuchs

gave names unto them: unto Daniel he gave the name of Belteshazzar; and to Hananiah, of Shadrach; and to Mishael, of Meshach; and to Azariah, of Abed-nego. But Daniel purposed in his heart that he would not defile himself with the king's meat, nor with the wine which he drank: therefore he requested of the prince of the eunuchs that he might not defile himself. Now God made Daniel to find favour and compassion in the sight of the prince of the eunuchs. And the prince of the eunuchs said unto Daniel, I fear my lord the king, who hath appointed your meat and your drink: for why should he see your faces worse liking than the youths which are of your own age? so should ye endanger my head with the king. Then said Daniel to the steward, whom the prince of the eunuchs had appointed over Daniel, Hananiah, Mishael, and Azariah: Prove thy servants, I beseech thee, ten days; and let them give us pulse to eat, and water to drink. Then let our countenances be looked upon before thee, and the countenance of the youths that eat of the king's meat; and as thou seest, deal with thy servants. So he hearkened unto them in this matter, and proved them ten days. And at the end of ten days their countenances appeared fairer, and they were fatter in flesh, than all the youths which did eat of the king's meat. So the steward took away their meat, and the wine that they should drink, and gave them pulse.

Now as for these four youths, God gave them knowledge

and skill in all learning and wisdom: and Daniel had understanding in all visions and dreams. And at the end of the days which the king had appointed for bringing them in, the prince of the eunuchs brought them in before Nebuchadnezzar. And the king communed with them; and among them all was found none like Daniel, Hananiah, · Mishael, and Azariah: therefore stood they before the king. And in every matter of wisdom and understanding, concerning which the king inquired of them, he found them ten times better than all the magicians and enchanters that were in all his realm. And Daniel continued even unto the first year of king Cyrus.

ii

The Dream of the Image and the Stone

And in the second year of the reign of Nebuchadnezzar Nebuchadnezzar dreamed dreams; and his spirit was troubled, and his sleep brake from him. Then the king commanded to call the magicians, and the enchanters, and the sorcerers, and the Chaldeans, for to tell the king his dreams. So they came in and stood before the king. And the king said unto them, I have dreamed a dream, and my spirit is troubled to know the dream. Then spake the Chaldeans to the king (in the Syrian* language), O king, live for ever: tell thy servants the dream, and we will shew the interpretation. The king answered and said to the Chaldeans, The thing is gone from me: if ye make not known unto me the dream and the interpretation thereof, ye shall be cut in pieces, and your houses shall be made a dunghill. But if ye shew the dream and the interpretation thereof, ye shall receive of me gifts and rewards and great honour: therefore shew me the dream and the interpretation thereof. They answered the second time and said, Let the king tell his servants the dream, and we will shew the interpretation. The king answered and said, I know of a certainty that ye would gain time, because ye see the thing is gone from me. But if ye make not known unto me the dream, there is but one law for you: for ye have prepared lying and corrupt words to speak before me, till the time be changed: therefore tell me the dream, and I shall know that ye can shew me the interpretation thereof. The Chaldeans answered before the king, and said, There is not a man upon the earth that can shew the king's matter: forasmuch as no king, lord, nor ruler, hath asked such a thing of any magician, or enchanter, or Chaldean. And it is a rare thing that the king requireth, and there is none other that can shew it before the king, except the gods, whose dwelling is not

* [From this point to the point marked on page 31 the language of the book is Aramaic instead of Hebrew.]

with flesh. For this cause the king was angry and very furious, and commanded to destroy all the wise men of Babylon. So the decree went forth, and the wise men were to be slain; and they sought Daniel and his companions to be slain. Then Daniel returned answer with counsel and prudence to Arioch the captain of the king's guard, which was gone forth to slay the wise men of Babylon; he answered and said to Arioch the king's captain, Wherefore is the decree so urgent from the king? Then Arioch made the thing known to Daniel. And Daniel went in, and desired of the king that he would appoint him a time, and he would shew the king the interpretation.

Then Daniel went to his house, and made the thing known to Hananiah, Mishael, and Azariah, his companions: that they would desire mercies of the God of heaven concerning this secret; that Daniel and his companions should not perish with the rest of the wise men of Babylon. Then was the secret revealed unto Daniel in a vision of the night. Then Daniel blessed the God of heaven. Daniel answered and said, Blessed be the name of God for ever and ever: for wisdom and might are his: and he changeth the times and the seasons: he removeth kings, and setteth up kings: he giveth wisdom unto the wise, and knowledge to them that know understanding: he revealeth the deep and secret things: he knoweth what is in the darkness, and the light dwelleth with him. I thank thee, and praise thee, O thou God of my fathers, who hast given me wisdom and might, and hast now made known unto me what we desired of thee: for thou hast made known unto us the king's matter. Therefore Daniel went in unto Arioch, whom the king had appointed to destroy the wise men of Babylon: he went and said thus unto him: Destroy not the wise men of Babylon: bring me in before the king, and I will shew unto the king the interpretation.

Then Arioch brought in Daniel before the king in haste, and said thus unto him, I have found a man of the children of the captivity of Judah, that will make known unto the king the interpretation. The king answered and said to Daniel (whose name was Belteshazzar), Art thou able to make known unto me the dream which I have seen, and the interpretation thereof? Daniel answered before the king, and said, The secret which the king hath demanded can neither wise men, enchanters, magicians, nor sooth-sayers, shew unto the king; but there is a God in heaven that revealeth secrets, and he hath made known to the king Nebuchadnezzar what shall be in the latter days. Thy dream, and the visions of thy head upon thy bed, are these: as for thee, O king, thy thoughts came into thy mind upon thy bed, what should come to pass hereafter: and he that revealeth secrets hath made known to thee what shall come to pass. But as for me, this secret is not revealed to me for any wisdom that I have more than any living, but to the intent that the interpretation may be made known to the king, and that thou mayest know the thoughts of thy heart.

Thou, O king, sawest, and behold a great image. This image, which was mighty, and whose brightness was excellent, stood before thee; and the aspect thereof was terrible. As for this image, his head was of fine gold, his breast and his arms of silver, his belly and his thighs of brass, his legs of iron, his feet part of iron, and part of clay. Thou sawest till that a stone was cut out without hands, which smote the image upon his feet that were of iron and clay, and brake them in pieces. Then was the iron, the clay, the brass, the silver, and the gold, broken in pieces together, and became like the chaff of the summer threshing-floors; and the wind carried them away, that no place was found for them: and the stone that smote the image became a great mountain, and filled the whole earth.

This is the dream; and we will tell the interpretation thereof before the king. Thou, O king, art king of kings, unto whom the God of heaven hath given the kingdom, the power, and the strength, and the glory; and wheresoever the children of men dwell, the beasts of the field and the fowls of the heaven hath he given into thine hand, and hath made thee to rule over them all: thou art the head of gold. And after thee shall arise another kingdom inferior to thee; and another third kingdom of brass, which shall bear rule over all the earth. And the fourth kingdom shall be strong as iron: forasmuch as iron breaketh in pieces and subdueth all things: and as iron that crusheth all these, shall it break in pieces and crush. And whereas thou sawest the feet and toes, part of potters' clay, and part of iron, it shall be a divided kingdom; but there shall be in it of the strength of the iron, forasmuch as thou sawest the iron mixed with miry clay. And as the toes of the feet were part of iron, and part of clay, so the kingdom shall be partly strong, and partly broken. And whereas thou sawest the iron mixed with miry clay, they shall mingle themselves with the seed of men; but they shall not cleave one to another, even as iron doth not mingle with clay. And in the days of those kings shall the God of heaven set up a kingdom, which shall never be destroyed, nor shall the sovereignty thereof be left to another people; but it shall break in pieces and consume all these kingdoms, and it shall stand for ever. Forasmuch as thou sawest that a stone was cut out of the mountain without hands, and that it brake in pieces the iron, the brass, the clay, the silver, and the gold; the great God hath made known to the king what shall come to pass hereafter: and the dream is certain, and the interpretation thereof sure.

Then the king Nebuchadnezzar fell upon his face, and worshipped Daniel, and commanded that they should offer an oblation and sweet odours unto him. The king answered unto Daniel, and said, Of a truth your God is the God of gods, and the Lord of kings, and a revealer of secrets, seeing thou hast been able to reveal this secret. Then the king made Daniel great, and gave him many great gifts, and made him to rule over the whole province of Babylon, and to be chief governor over all the wise men of Babylon. And Daniel requested of the king, and he appointed Shadrach, Meshach, and Abed-nego, over the affairs of the province of Babylon: but Daniel was in the gate of the king.

iii

The Story of Shadrach, Meshach, and Abed-nego

Nebuchadnezzar the king made an image of gold, whose height was threescore cubits, and the breadth thereof six cubits: he set it up in the plain of Dura, in the province of Babylon. Then Nebuchadnezzar the king sent to gather together the satraps, the deputies, and the governors, the judges, the treasurers, the counsellors, the sheriffs, and all the rulers of the provinces, to come to the dedication of the image which Nebuchadnezzar the king had set up. Then the satraps, the deputies, and the governors, the judges, the treasurers, the counsellors, the sheriffs, and all the rulers of the provinces, were gathered together unto the dedication of the image that Nebuchadnezzar the king had set up; and they stood before the image that Nebuchadnezzar had set up. Then the herald cried aloud, To you it is commanded, O peoples, nations, and languages, that at what time ye hear the sound of the cornet, flute, harp, sackbut, psaltery, dulcimer, and all kinds of music, ye fall down and worship the golden image that Nebuchadnezzar the king hath set up: and whoso falleth not down and worshippeth shall the same hour be cast into the midst of a burning fiery furnace. Therefore at that time, when all the peoples heard the sound of the cornet, flute, harp, sackbut, psaltery, and all kinds of music, all the peoples, the nations, and the languages, fell down and worshipped the golden image that Nebuchadnezzar the king had set up.

Wherefore at that time certain Chaldeans came near, and brought accusation against the Jews. They answered and said to Nebuchadnezzar the king: O king, live for ever. Thou, O king, hast made a decree, that every man that shall hear the sound of the cornet, flute, harp, sackbut, psaltery, and dulcimer, and all kinds of music, shall fall down and worship the golden image: and whoso falleth not down and worshippeth, shall be cast into the midst of a burning fiery furnace. There are certain Jews whom thou hast appointed over the affairs of the province of Babylon, Shadrach, Meshach, and Abed-nego; these men, O king, have not regarded thee: they serve not thy gods, nor worship the golden image which thou hast set up. Then Nebuchadnezzar in his rage and fury commanded to bring Shadrach, Meshach, and Abed-nego. Then they brought these men before the king. Nebuchadnezzar answered and said unto them, Is it of purpose, O Shadrach, Meshach,

and Abed-nego, that ye serve not my god, nor worship
the golden image which I have set up? Now if ye be
ready that at what time ye hear the sound of the cornet,
flute, harp, sackbut, psaltery, and dulcimer, and all kinds
of music, ye fall down and worship the image which I have
made, well: but if ye worship not, ye shall be cast the
same hour into the midst of a burning fiery furnace; and
who is that god that shall deliver you out of my hands?
Shadrach, Meshach, and Abed-nego, answered and said to
the king, O Nebuchadnezzar, we have no need to answer
thee in this matter. If it be so, our God whom we serve is
able to deliver us from the burning fiery furnace; and he
will deliver us out of thine hand, O king. But if not, be
it known unto thee, O king, that we will not serve thy
gods, nor worship the golden image which thou hast set up.
Then was Nebuchadnezzar full of fury, and the form of his
visage was changed against Shadrach, Meshach, and Abed-
nego: therefore he spake, and commanded that they should
heat the furnace seven times more than it was wont to be
heated. And he commanded certain mighty men that were
in his army to bind Shadrach, Meshach, and Abed-nego,
and to cast them into the burning fiery furnace. Then
these men were bound in their hosen, their tunics, and
their mantles, and their other garments, and were cast into
the midst of the burning fiery furnace. Therefore because
the king's commandment was urgent, and the furnace exceeding hot, the flame of the fire slew those men that took up

Shadrach, Meshach, and Abed-nego.   And these three men, Shadrach, Meshach, and Abed-nego, fell down bound into the midst of the burning fiery furnace.

Then Nebuchadnezzar the king was astonied, and rose up in haste: he spake and said unto his counsellors, Did not we cast three men bound into the midst of the fire? They answered and said unto the king, True, O king.   He answered and said, Lo, I see four men loose, walking in the midst of the fire, and they have no hurt; and the aspect of the fourth is like a son of the gods.   Then Nebuchadnezzar came near to the mouth of the burning fiery furnace: he spake and said, Shadrach, Meshach, and Abednego, ye servants of the Most High God, come forth, and come hither.   Then Shadrach, Meshach, and Abednego, came forth out of the midst of the fire.   And the satraps, the deputies, and the governors, and the king's counsellors, being gathered together, saw these men, that the fire had no power upon their bodies, nor was the hair of their head singed, neither were their hosen changed, nor had the smell of fire passed on them.   Nebuchadnezzar spake and said: Blessed be the God of Shadrach, Meshach, and Abed-nego, who hath sent his angel, and delivered his servants that trusted in him, and have changed the king's word, and have yielded their bodies, that they might not serve nor worship any god, except their own God.   Therefore I make a decree, that every people, nation, and language, which speak any thing amiss against the God of Shadrach,

Meshach, and Abed-nego, shall be cut in pieces, and their houses shall be made a dunghill: because there is no other god that is able to deliver after this sort. Then the king promoted Shadrach, Meshach, and Abed-nego, in the province of Babylon.

iv

The Dream of the Tree that was cut down

'Nebuchadnezzar the king, unto all the peoples, nations, and languages, that dwell in all the earth: peace be multiplied unto you. It hath seemed good unto me to shew the signs and wonders that the Most High God hath wrought toward me. How great are his signs! and how mighty are his wonders! his kingdom is an everlasting kingdom, and his dominion is from generation to generation.

'I Nebuchadnezzar was at rest in mine house, and flourishing in my palace. I saw a dream which made me afraid; and the thoughts upon my bed and the visions of my head troubled me. Therefore made I a decree to bring in all the wise men of Babylon before me, that they might make known unto me the interpretation of the dream. Then came in the magicians, the enchanters, the Chaldeans, and the soothsayers: and I told the dream before them; but they did not make known unto me the interpretation thereof. But at the last Daniel came in before me, whose name was Belteshazzar, according to the name of my god, and in whom is the spirit of the holy gods: and I told the dream before him, saying, O Belteshazzar, master of the magicians, because I know that the spirit of the holy gods is in thee, and no secret troubleth thee, tell me the visions of my dream that I have seen, and the interpretation thereof.

'Thus were the visions of my head upon my bed: I saw, and behold a tree in the midst of the earth, and the height thereof was great. The tree grew, and was strong, and the height thereof reached unto heaven, and the sight thereof to the end of all the earth. The leaves thereof were fair, and the fruit thereof much, and in it was meat for all: the beasts of the field had shadow under it, and the fowls of the heaven dwelt in the branches thereof, and all flesh was fed of it. I saw in the visions of my head upon my bed, and, behold, a watcher and an holy one came down from heaven. He cried aloud, and said thus: "Hew down the tree, and cut off his branches, shake off his leaves, and scatter his fruit: let the beasts get away from under it, and the fowls from his branches. Nevertheless leave the stump of his roots in the earth, even with a band of iron and brass, in the tender grass of the field; and let it be wet with the dew of heaven, and let his portion be with the beasts in the grass of the earth: let his heart be changed from man's, and let a beast's heart be given unto him; and let seven times pass over him. The sentence is by the decree of the watchers, and the demand by the word of the holy ones: to the intent that the living may know that the Most High ruleth in the kingdom of men, and giveth it to whomsoever he will, and setteth up over it the lowest of men." This dream I king Nebuchadnezzar have seen: and thou, O Belteshazzar, declare the interpretation, forasmuch as all the wise men of my kingdom are not able to make known unto me the interpretation; but thou art able, for the spirit of the holy gods is in thee.

'Then Daniel, whose name was Belteshazzar, was astonied for a while, and his thoughts troubled him. The king answered and said, Belteshazzar, let not the dream, or the interpretation, trouble thee. Belteshazzar answered and said, My lord, the dream be to them that hate thee, and the interpretation thereof to thine adversaries. The tree that thou sawest, which grew, and was strong, whose height reached unto the heaven, and the sight thereof to all the earth; whose leaves were fair, and the fruit thereof much, and in it was meat for all; under which the beasts of the field dwelt, and upon whose branches the fowls of the heaven had their habitation; it is thou, O king, that art grown and become strong: for thy greatness is grown, and reacheth unto heaven, and thy dominion to the end of the earth. And whereas the king saw a watcher and an holy one coming down from heaven, and saying, Hew down the tree, and destroy it; nevertheless leave the

stump of the roots thereof in the earth, even with a band
of iron and brass, in the tender grass of the field; and let
it be wet with the dew of heaven, and let his portion be
with the beasts of the field, till seven times pass over him;
this is the interpretation, O king, and it is the decree of
the Most High, which is come upon my lord the king:
that thou shalt be driven from men, and thy dwelling shall
be with the beasts of the field, and thou shalt be made to
eat grass as oxen, and shalt be wet with the dew of heaven,
and seven times shall pass over thee; till thou know that
the Most High ruleth in the kingdom of men, and giveth
it to whomsoever he will. And whereas they commanded to
leave the stump of the tree roots; thy kingdom shall be
sure unto thee, after that thou shalt have known that the
heavens do rule. Wherefore, O king, let my counsel be
acceptable unto thee, and break off thy sins by righteousness, and thine iniquities by shewing mercy to the poor;
if there may be a lengthening of thy tranquillity.

'All this came upon the king Nebuchadnezzar. At the
end of twelve months he was walking in the royal palace
of Babylon. The king spake and said, Is not this great
Babylon, which I have built for the royal dwelling place,
by the might of my power and for the glory of my majesty? While the word was in the king's mouth, there
fell a voice from heaven, saying: "O king Nebuchadnezzar,
to thee it is spoken: the kingdom is departed from thee.
And thou shalt be driven from men, and thy dwelling

shall be with the beasts of the field; thou shalt be made to eat grass as oxen, and seven times shall pass over thee; until thou know that the Most High ruleth in the kingdom of men, and giveth it to whomsoever he will." The same hour was the thing fulfilled upon Nebuchadnezzar: and he was driven from men, and did eat grass as oxen, and his body was wet with the dew of heaven, till his hair was grown like eagles' feathers, and his nails like birds' claws. And at the end of the days I Nebuchadnezzar lifted up mine eyes unto heaven, and mine understanding returned unto me, and I blessed the Most High, and I praised and honoured him that liveth for ever; for his dominion is an everlasting dominion, and his kingdom from generation to generation: and all the inhabitants of the earth are reputed as nothing: and he doeth according to his will in the army of heaven, and among the inhabitants of the earth: and none can stay his hand, or say unto him, What doest thou? At the same time mine understanding returned unto me; and for the glory of my kingdom, my majesty and brightness returned unto me; and my counsellors and my lords sought unto me; and I was established in my kingdom, and excellent greatness was added unto me.

'Now I Nebuchadnezzar praise and extol and honour the King of heaven; for all his works are truth, and his ways judgement: and those that walk in pride he is able to abase.'

V

The Story of Belshazzar's Feast

Belshazzar the king made a great feast to a thousand of his lords, and drank wine before the thousand. Belshazzar, whiles he tasted the wine, commanded to bring the golden and silver vessels which Nebuchadnezzar his father had taken out of the temple which was in Jerusalem; that the king and his lords, his wives and his concubines, might drink therein. Then they brought the golden vessels that were taken out of the temple of the house of God which was at Jerusalem; and the king and his lords, his wives and his concubines, drank in them. They drank wine, and praised the gods of gold, and of silver, of brass, of iron, of wood, and of stone. In the same hour came forth the fingers of a man's hand, and wrote over against the candlestick upon the plaister of the wall of the king's palace: and the king saw the part of the hand that wrote. Then the king's countenance was changed in him, and his thoughts troubled him; and the joints of his loins were loosed, and his knees smote one against another. The king cried aloud to bring in the enchanters, the Chaldeans, and the soothsayers. The king spake and said to the wise men of Babylon, Whosoever shall read this writing, and shew me the interpretation thereof, shall be clothed with purple, and have a chain of gold about his neck, and shall rule as one of three in the kingdom. Then came in all the king's wise men : but they could not read the writing, nor make known to the king the interpretation. Then was king Belshazzar greatly troubled, and his countenance was changed in him, and his lords were perplexed.

Now the queen by reason of the words of the king and his lords came into the banquet house : the queen spake and said : O king, live for ever; let not thy thoughts trouble thee, nor let thy countenance be changed : there is a man in thy kingdom, in whom is the spirit of the holy gods ; and in the days of thy father light and understanding and wisdom, like the wisdom of the gods, was found in him : and the king Nebuchadnezzar thy father, the king, I say, thy father, made him master of the magicians, enchanters, Chaldeans, and soothsayers ; forasmuch as an excellent spirit, and knowledge, and understanding, interpreting of dreams, and shewing of dark sentences, and dissolving of doubts, were found in the same Daniel, whom the king named Belteshazzar. Now let Daniel be called, and he will shew the interpretation.

Then was Daniel brought in before the king. The king spake and said unto Daniel, Art thou that Daniel, which art of the children of the captivity of Judah, whom the king my father brought out of Judah? I have heard of thee, that the spirit of the gods is in thee, and that light and understanding and excellent wisdom is found in thee. And now the wise men, the enchanters, have been brought in before me, that they should read this writing, and make known unto me the interpretation thereof: but they could not shew the interpretation of the thing. But I have heard of thee, that thou canst give interpretations, and dissolve doubts: now if thou canst read the writing, and make known to me the interpretation thereof, thou shalt be clothed with purple, and have a chain of gold about thy neck, and shalt rule as one of three in the kingdom. Then Daniel answered and said before the king: Let thy gifts be to thyself, and give thy rewards to another; nevertheless I will read the writing unto the king, and make known to him the interpretation. O thou king, the Most High God gave Nebuchadnezzar thy father the kingdom, and greatness, and glory, and majesty: and because of the greatness that he gave him, all the peoples, nations, and languages trembled and feared before him: whom he would he slew, and whom he would he kept alive; and whom he would he raised up, and whom he would he put down. But when his heart was lifted up, and his spirit was hardened that he dealt proudly, he was deposed from his kingly throne, and they took his glory from him: and he was driven from the sons of men; and his heart was made like the beasts, and his dwelling was with the wild asses; he was fed with grass like oxen, and his body was wet with the dew of heaven: until he knew that the Most High God ruleth in the kingdom of men, and

that he setteth up over it whomsoever he will. And thou
his son, O Belshazzar, hast not humbled thine heart,
though thou knewest all this; but hast lifted up thyself
against the Lord of heaven; and they have brought the
vessels of his house before thee, and thou and thy lords,
thy wives and thy concubines have drunk wine in them;
and thou hast praised the gods of silver, and gold, of brass,
iron, wood, and stone, which see not, nor hear, nor know:
and the God in whose hand thy breath is, and whose are
all thy ways, hast thou not glorified: then was the part of
the hand sent from before him, and this writing was
inscribed. And this is the writing that was inscribed *:

M	A	P
E	L	H
N	E	A
E	K	R
M	E	S
E	T	I
N	E	N

This is the interpretation of the thing:

MENE

God hath NUMBERED thy kingdom:
And brought it to an end !

* [Daniel reads down, up, down: instead of across.]

23

TEKEL

Thou art WEIGHED in the balances:
And art found wanting!

PERES

Thy kingdom is DIVIDED
And given to the Medes and Persians!

Then commanded Belshazzar, and they clothed Daniel with purple, and put a chain of gold about his neck, and made proclamation concerning him, that he should rule as one of three in the kingdom. In that night Belshazzar the Chaldean king was slain. And Darius the Mede received the kingdom, being about threescore and two years old.

vi

The Story of Daniel in the Den of Lions

It pleased Darius to set over the kingdom an hundred and twenty satraps, which should be throughout the whole kingdom; and over them three presidents, of whom Daniel was one; that these satraps might give account unto them, and that the king should have no damage. Then this Daniel was distinguished above the presidents and the satraps, because an excellent spirit was in him; and the king thought to set him over the whole realm.

Then the presidents and the satraps sought to find occasion against Daniel as touching the kingdom; but they could find none occasion nor fault; forasmuch as he was faithful, neither was there any error or fault found in him. Then said these men, We shall not find any occasion against this Daniel, except we find it against him concerning the law of his God. Then these presidents and satraps assembled together to the king, and said thus unto him: King Darius, live for ever. All the presidents of the kingdom, the deputies and the satraps, the counsellors and the governors, have consulted together to establish a royal statute, and to make a strong interdict, that whosoever shall ask a petition of any god or man for thirty days, save of thee, O king, he shall be cast into the den of lions. Now, O king, establish the interdict, and sign the writing, that it be not changed, according to the law of the Medes and Persians, which altereth not. Wherefore king Darius signed the writing and the interdict.

And when Daniel knew that the writing was signed, he went into his house; (now his windows were open in his chamber toward Jerusalem;) and he kneeled upon his knees three times a day, and prayed, and gave thanks before his God, as he did aforetime. Then these men assembled together, and found Daniel making petition and supplication before his God. Then they came near, and spake before the king concerning the king's interdict: Hast thou not signed an interdict, that every man that shall make petition unto any god or man within thirty days, save unto thee, O king, shall be cast into the den of lions? The king answered and said, The thing is true, according to the law of the Medes and Persians, which altereth not. Then answered they and said before the king, That Daniel, which is of the children of the captivity of Judah, regardeth not thee, O king, nor the interdict that thou hast signed, but maketh his petition three times a day. Then the king, when he heard these words, was sore displeased, and set his heart on Daniel to deliver him: and he laboured till the going down of the sun to rescue him. Then these men assembled together unto the king, and said unto the king, Know, O king, that it is a law of the Medes and Persians, that no interdict nor statute which the king establisheth may be changed. Then the king commanded, and they brought Daniel and cast him into the den of lions. Now the king spake and said unto Daniel, Thy God whom thou servest continually, he will deliver thee. And a stone was brought, and laid upon the mouth of the den; and the king sealed it with his own signet, and with the signet of his lords; that nothing might be changed concerning Daniel.

Then the king went to his palace, and passed the night fasting; neither were instruments of music brought before him; and his sleep fled from him. Then the king arose

26

very early in the morning, and went in haste unto the den of lions. And when he came near unto the den to Daniel, he cried with a lamentable voice: the king spake and said to Daniel, O Daniel, servant of the living God, is thy God, whom thou servest continually, able to deliver thee from the lions? Then said Daniel unto the king, O king, live for ever. My God hath sent his angel, and hath shut the lions' mouths, and they have not hurt me: forasmuch as before him innocency was found in me; and also before thee, O king, have I done no hurt. Then was the king exceeding glad, and commanded that they should take Daniel up out of the den. So Daniel was taken up out of the den, and no manner of hurt was found upon him, because he had trusted in his God. And the king commanded, and they brought those men which had accused Daniel, and they cast them into the den of lions, them, their children, and their wives; and the lions had the mastery of them, and brake all their bones in pieces, or ever they came at the bottom of the den.

Then king Darius wrote unto all the peoples, nations, and languages, that dwell in all the earth: *Peace be multiplied unto you. I make a decree, that in all the dominion of my kingdom men tremble and fear before the God of Daniel: for he is the living God, and stedfast for ever, and his kingdom that which shall not be destroyed, and his dominion shall be even unto the end: he delivereth and rescueth, and he worketh signs and wonders in heaven and in earth; who hath delivered Daniel from the power of the lions.*

So this Daniel prospered in the reign of Darius, and in the reign of Cyrus the Persian.

vii

THE REVELATION OF DANIEL

The Vision of the Four Beasts

In the first year of Belshazzar king of Babylon Daniel had a dream and visions of his head upon his bed: then he wrote the dream and told the sum of the matters. Daniel spake and said: I saw in my vision by night, and, behold, the four winds of the heaven brake forth upon the great sea. And four great beasts came up from the sea, diverse one from another. The first was like a lion, and had eagle's wings: I beheld till the wings thereof were plucked, and it was lifted up from the earth, and made to stand upon two feet as a man, and a man's heart was given to it. And behold another beast, a second, like to a bear, and it was raised up on one side, and three ribs were in his mouth between his teeth: and they said thus unto it, Arise, devour much flesh. After this I beheld, and lo

28

another, like a leopard, which had upon the back of it four wings of a fowl; the beast had also four heads; and dominion was given to it. After this I saw in the night visions, and behold a fourth beast, terrible and powerful, and strong exceedingly; and it had great iron teeth: it devoured and brake in pieces, and stamped the residue with his feet: and it was diverse from all the beasts that were before it; and it had ten horns. I considered the horns, and, behold, there came up among them another horn, a little one, before which three of the first horns were plucked up by the roots: and, behold, in this horn were eyes like the eyes of a man, and a mouth speaking great things. I beheld till thrones were placed, and one that was ancient of days did sit: his raiment was white as snow, and the hair of his head like pure wool; his throne was fiery flames, and the wheels thereof burning fire. A fiery stream issued and came forth from before him: thousand thousands ministered unto him, and ten thousand times ten thousand stood before him: the judgement was set, and the books were opened. I beheld at that time because of the voice of the great words which the horn spake; I beheld even till the beast was slain, and his body destroyed, and he was given to be burned with fire. And as for the rest of the beasts, their dominion was taken away: yet their lives were prolonged for a season and a time. I saw in the night visions, and, behold, there came with the clouds of heaven one like unto a son of man, and he came even to the ancient of days, and they brought him near before him. And there was given him dominion, and glory, and a kingdom, that all the peoples, nations, and languages should serve him: his dominion is an everlasting dominion, which shall not pass away, and his kingdom that which shall not be destroyed.

As for me Daniel, my spirit was grieved in the midst of my body, and the visions of my head troubled me. I came near unto one of them that stood by, and asked him the truth concerning all this. So he told me, and made me know the interpretation of the things. These great beasts, which are four, are four kings, which shall arise out of the earth. But the saints of the Most High shall receive the kingdom, and possess the kingdom for ever, even for ever and ever. Then I desired to know the truth concerning the fourth beast, which was diverse from all of them, exceedingly terrible, whose teeth were of iron, and his nails of brass; which devoured, brake in pieces, and stamped the residue with his feet: and concerning the ten horns that were on his head, and the other horn which came up, and before which three fell; even that horn that had eyes, and a mouth that spake great things, whose look was more stout than his fellows. I beheld, and the same horn made war with the saints, and prevailed against them; until the ancient of days came, and judgment was given to the saints of the Most High; and the time came that the saints possessed the kingdom. Thus he said,

The fourth beast shall be a fourth kingdom upon earth, which shall be diverse from all the kingdoms, and shall devour the whole earth, and shall tread it down, and break it in pieces. And as for the ten horns, out of this kingdom shall ten kings arise: and another shall arise after them; and he shall be diverse from the former, and he shall put down three kings. And he shall speak words against the Most High, and shall wear out the saints of the Most High: and he shall think to change the times and the law; and they shall be given into his hand until a time and times and half a time. But the judgement shall sit, and they shall take away his dominion, to consume and to destroy it unto the end. And the kingdom and the dominion, and the greatness of the kingdoms under the whole heaven, shall be given to the people of the saints of the Most High: his kingdom is an everlasting kingdom, and all dominions shall serve and obey him. Here is the end of the matter. As for me Daniel, my thoughts much troubled me, and my countenance was changed in me: but I kept the matter in my heart.

2 *

The Vision of the Ram and the He-goat

In the third year of the reign of king Belshazzar a vision appeared unto me, even unto me Daniel, after that which

* [From this point to the end Hebrew is resumed in the original.]

appeared unto me at the first. And I saw in the vision—
now it was so, that when I saw, I was in Shushan the
palace, which is in the province of Elam—and I saw in
the vision, and I was by the river Ulai. Then I lifted up
mine eyes, and saw, and, behold, there stood before the
river a ram which had two horns: and the two horns were
high; but one was higher than the other, and the higher
came up last. I saw the ram pushing westward, and north-
ward, and southward; and no beasts could stand before
him, neither was there any that could deliver out of his
hand; but he did according to his will, and magnified
himself. And as I was considering, behold, an he-goat
came from the west over the face of the whole earth, and
touched not the ground: and the goat had a notable horn
between his eyes. And he came to the ram that had the
two horns, which I saw standing before the river, and ran
upon him in the fury of his power. And I saw him come
close unto the ram, and he was moved with choler against
him, and smote the ram, and brake his two horns; and
there was no power in the ram to stand before him: but
he cast him down to the ground, and trampled upon him;
and there was none that could deliver the ram out of his
hand. And the he-goat magnified himself exceedingly:
and when he was strong, the great horn was broken; and
instead of it there came up four notable horns toward the
four winds of heaven. And out of one of them came forth
a little horn, which waxed exceeding great, toward the

south, and toward the east, and toward the glorious land. And it waxed great, even to the host of heaven; and some of the host and of the stars it cast down to the ground, and trampled upon them. Yea, it magnified itself, even to the prince of the host; and it took away from him the continual burnt offering, and the place of his sanctuary was cast down. And the host was given over to it together with the continual burnt offering through transgression; and it cast down truth to the ground, and it did its pleasure and prospered. Then I heard a holy one speaking; and another holy one said unto that certain one which spake: How long shall be the vision concerning the continual burnt offering, and the transgression that maketh desolate, to give both the sanctuary and the host to be trodden under foot? And he said unto me: Unto two thousand and three hundred evenings and mornings; then shall the sanctuary be cleansed.

And it came to pass, when I, even I Daniel, had seen the vision, that I sought to understand it; and, behold, there stood before me as the appearance of a man. And I heard a man's voice between the banks of Ulai, which called, and said, Gabriel, make this man to understand the vision. So he came near where I stood; and when he came, I was affrighted, and fell upon my face: but he said unto me, Understand, O son of man; for the vision belongeth to the time of the end. Now as he was speaking with me, I fell into a deep sleep with my face toward the ground: but he touched me, and set me upright. And he said, Behold, I will make thee know what shall be in the latter time of the indignation: for it belongeth to the appointed time of the end. The ram which thou sawest that had the two horns, they are the kings of Media and Persia. And the rough he-goat is the king of Greece: and the great horn that is between his eyes is the first king. And as for that which was broken, in the place whereof four stood up, four kingdoms shall stand up out of the nation, but not with his power. And in the latter time of their kingdom, when the transgressors are come to the full, a king of fierce countenance, and understanding dark sentences, shall stand up. And his power shall be mighty, but not by his own power; and he shall destroy wonderfully, and shall prosper and do his pleasure: and he shall destroy the mighty ones and the holy people. And through his policy he shall cause craft to prosper in his hand; and he shall magnify himself in his heart, and in their security shall he destroy many: he shall also stand up against the prince of princes; but he shall be broken without hand. And the vision of the evenings and mornings which hath been told is true: but shut thou up the vision; for it belongeth to many days to come. And I Daniel fainted, and was sick certain days; then I rose up, and did the king's business: and I was astonished at the vision, but there was none to make it understood.

Daniel ✎

3

Vision of the Time of Restoration

In the first year of Darius the son of Ahasuerus, of the seed of the Medes, which was made king over the realm of the Chaldeans; in the first year of his reign I Daniel understood by the books the number of the years, whereof the word of the LORD came to Jeremiah the prophet, for the accomplishing of the desolations of Jerusalem, even seventy years. And I set my face unto the Lord God, to seek by prayer and supplications, with fasting, and sackcloth, and ashes. And I prayed unto the LORD my God, and made confession, and said:

'O Lord, the great and dreadful God, which keepeth covenant and mercy with them that love him and keep his commandments; we have sinned, and have dealt perversely, and have done wickedly, and have rebelled, even turning aside from thy precepts and from thy judgements: neither have we hearkened unto thy servants the prophets, which spake in thy name to our kings, our princes, and our fathers, and to all the people of the land. O Lord, righteousness belongeth unto thee, but unto us confusion of face, as at this day; to the men of Judah, and to the inhabitants of Jerusalem, and unto all Israel, that are near, and that are far off, through all the countries whither thou hast driven them, because of their trespass that they have trespassed against thee. O Lord, to us belongeth confusion of face, to our kings, to our princes, and to our fathers, because we have sinned against thee. To the Lord our God belong mercies and forgivenesses; for we have rebelled against him; neither have we obeyed the voice of the LORD our God, to walk in his laws, which he set before us by his servants the prophets. Yea, all Israel have transgressed thy law, even turning aside, that they should not obey thy voice: therefore hath the curse been poured out upon us, and the oath that is written in the law of Moses the servant of God; for we have sinned against him. And he hath confirmed his words, which he spake against us, and against our judges that judged us, by bringing upon us a great evil: for under the whole heaven hath not been done as hath been done upon Jerusalem. As it is written in the law of Moses, all this evil is come upon us: yet have we not intreated the favour of the LORD our God, that we should turn from our iniquities, and have discernment in thy truth. Therefore hath the LORD watched over the evil, and brought it upon us: for the LORD our God is righteous in all his works which he doeth, and we have not obeyed his voice. And now, O Lord our God, that hast brought thy people forth out of the land of Egypt with a mighty hand, and hast gotten thee renown, as at this day; we have sinned, we have done wickedly. O Lord, according to all thy righteousness, let thine anger and thy fury, I pray thee, be turned away from thy city Jerusalem, thy holy mountain: because for our sins, and for the iniquities of our fathers, Jerusalem and thy people are become a reproach to all that are round about us. Now therefore, O our God, hearken unto the prayer of thy servant, and to his supplications, and cause thy face to shine upon thy sanctuary that is desolate, for the Lord's sake. O my God, incline thine ear, and hear; open thine eyes, and behold our desolations, and the city which is called by thy name: for we do not present our supplications before thee for our righteousnesses, but for thy great mercies. O Lord, hear; O Lord, forgive; O Lord, hearken and do; defer not; for thine own sake, O my God, because thy city and thy people are called by thy name.'

And whiles I was speaking, and praying, and confessing my sin and the sin of my people Israel, and presenting my supplication before the LORD my God for the holy mountain of my God; yea, whiles I was speaking in prayer, the man Gabriel, whom I had seen in the vision at the beginning, being caused to fly swiftly, touched me about the time of the evening oblation. And he instructed me, and talked with me, and said, O Daniel, I am now come forth to make thee skilful of understanding. At the beginning of thy supplications the commandment went forth, and I am come to tell thee; for thou art greatly beloved: therefore consider the matter, and understand the vision. Seventy weeks are decreed upon thy people and upon thy holy city, to finish transgression, and to make an end of sins, and to make reconciliation for iniquity, and to bring in everlasting righteousness, and to seal up vision and prophecy, and to anoint the most holy. Know therefore and discern, that from the going forth of the commandment to restore and to build Jerusalem unto the anointed one, the prince, shall be seven weeks: and threescore and two weeks, it shall be built again, with street and moat, even in troublous times. And after the threescore and two weeks shall the anointed one be cut off, and shall have nothing: and the people of the prince that shall come shall destroy the city and the sanctuary; and his end shall be with a flood, and even unto the end shall be war; desolations are determined. And he shall make a firm covenant with many for one week: and for the half of the week he shall cause the sacrifice and the oblation to cease; and upon the wing of abominations shall come one that maketh desolate; and even unto the consummation, and that determined, shall wrath be poured out upon the desolator.

4

Vision of the Time of the End

In the third year of Cyrus king of Persia a thing was revealed unto Daniel, whose name was called Belteshazzar; and the thing was true, even a great warfare: and he understood the thing, and had understanding of the vision. In those days I Daniel was mourning three whole weeks.

Daniel ✎

I ate no pleasant bread, neither came flesh nor wine in my mouth, neither did I anoint myself at all, till three whole weeks were fulfilled. And in the four and twentieth day of the first month, as I was by the side of the great river, which is Hiddekel, I lifted up mine eyes, and looked, and behold a man clothed in linen, whose loins were girded with pure gold of Uphaz: his body also was like the beryl, and his face as the appearance of lightning, and his eyes as lamps of fire, and his arms and his feet like in colour to burnished brass, and the voice of his words like the voice of a multitude. And I Daniel alone saw the vision: for the men that were with me saw not the vision; but a great quaking fell upon them, and they fled to hide themselves. So I was left alone, and saw this great vision, and there remained no strength in me: for my comeliness was turned in me into corruption, and I retained no strength. Yet heard I the voice of his words: and when I heard the voice of his words, then was I fallen into a deep sleep on my face, with my face toward the ground. And, behold, a hand touched me, which set me upon my knees and upon the palms of my hands. And he said unto me, O Daniel, thou man greatly beloved, understand the words that I speak unto thee, and stand upright; for unto thee am I now sent: and when he had spoken this word unto me, I stood trembling. Then said he unto me, Fear not, Daniel; for from the first day that thou didst set thine heart to understand, and to humble thyself before thy God, thy words were heard: and I am come for thy words' sake. But the prince of the kingdom of Persia withstood me one and twenty days; but, lo, Michael, one of the chief princes, came to help me: and I remained there with the kings of Persia. Now I am come to make thee understand what shall befall thy people in the latter days: for the vision is yet for many days. And when he had spoken unto me according to these words, I set my face toward the ground, and was dumb. And, behold, one like the similitude of the sons of men touched my lips: then I opened my mouth, and spake and said unto him that stood before me, O my lord, by reason of the vision my sorrows are turned upon me, and I retain no strength. For how can the servant of this my lord talk with this my lord? for as for me, straightway there remained no strength in me, neither was there breath left in me. Then there touched me again one like the appearance of a man, and he strengthened me. And he said, O man greatly beloved, fear not: peace be unto thee, be strong, yea, be strong. And when he spake unto me, I was strengthened, and said, Let my lord speak; for thou hast strengthened me. Then said he, Knowest thou wherefore I am come unto thee? and now will I return to fight with the prince of Persia: and when I go forth, lo, the prince of Greece shall come. But I will tell thee that which is inscribed in the writing of truth: and there is none that holdeth with me against these, but Michael your prince. And as for me, in the first year of Darius the Mede, I stood up to confirm and strengthen him.

And now will I shew thee the truth. Behold, there shall stand up yet three kings in Persia; and the fourth shall be far richer than they all: and when he is waxed strong through his riches, he shall stir up all against the realm of Greece. And a mighty king shall stand up, that shall rule with great dominion, and do according to his will. And when he shall stand up, his kingdom shall be broken, and shall be divided toward the four winds of heaven; but not to his posterity, nor according to his dominion wherewith he ruled; for his kingdom shall be plucked up, even for others beside these. And the king of the south shall be strong, and one of his princes; and he shall be strong above him, and have dominion; his dominion shall be a great dominion. And at the end of years they shall join themselves together; and the daughter of the king of the south shall come to the king of the north to make an agreement: but she shall not retain the strength of her arm; neither shall he stand, nor his arm; but she shall be given up, and they that brought her, and he that begat her, and he that strengthened her in those times. But out of a shoot from her roots shall one stand up in his place, which shall come unto the army, and shall enter into the fortress of the king of the north, and shall deal against them, and shall prevail: and also their gods, with their molten images, and with their goodly vessels of silver and of gold, shall he carry captive into Egypt; and he shall refrain some years from the king of the north. And he shall come into the realm of the king of the south, but he shall return into his own land. And his sons shall war, and shall assemble a multitude of great forces, which shall come on, and overflow, and pass through: and they shall return and war, even to his fortress. And the king of the south shall be moved with choler, and shall come forth and fight with him, even with the king of the north: and he shall set forth a great multitude, and the multitude shall be given into his hand. And the multitude shall be lifted up, and his heart shall be exalted: and he shall cast down tens of thousands, but he shall not prevail. And the king of the north shall return, and shall set forth a multitude greater than the former; and he shall come on at the end of the times, even of years, with a great army and with much substance. And in those times there shall many stand up against the king of the south: also the children of the violent among thy people shall lift themselves up to establish the vision; but they shall fall. So the king of the north shall come, and cast up a mount, and take a well fenced city: and the arms of the south shall not withstand, neither his chosen people, neither shall there be any strength to withstand. But he that cometh against him shall do according to his own will, and none shall stand before him: and he shall stand in the glorious land, and in his hand shall be destruction. And he shall set his face to come with the strength of his whole kingdom, and upright ones with him; and he shall do his pleasure: and he shall give him the daughter of women, to corrupt her; but she shall not stand, neither be for him. After this shall he turn his face unto the isles, and shall take many: but a prince shall cause the reproach offered by him to cease; yea, moreover, he shall cause his reproach to turn upon him. Then he shall turn his face toward the fortresses of his own land: but he shall stumble and fall, and shall not be found. Then shall stand up in his place one that shall cause an exactor to pass through the glory of the kingdom: but within few days he shall be destroyed, neither in anger, nor in battle. And in his place shall stand up a contemptible person, to whom they had not given the honour of the kingdom: but he shall come in time of security, and shall obtain the kingdom by flatteries. And with the arms of a flood shall they be swept away from before him, and shall be broken; yea, also the prince of the covenant. And after the league made with him he shall work deceitfully: for he shall come up, and shall become strong, with a small people. In time of security shall he come even upon the fattest places of the province; and he shall do that which his fathers have not done, nor his fathers' fathers; he shall scatter among them prey, and spoil, and substance: yea, he shall devise his devices against the strong holds, even for a time. And he shall stir up his power and his courage against the king of the south with a great army; and the king of the south shall war in battle with an exceeding great and mighty army: but he shall not stand, for they shall devise devices against him. Yea, they that eat of his meat shall destroy him, and his army shall overflow; and many shall fall down slain. And as for both these kings, their hearts shall be to do mischief, and they shall speak lies at one table: but it shall not prosper; for yet the end shall be at the time appointed. Then shall he return into his land with great substance; and his heart shall be against the holy covenant; and he shall do his pleasure, and return to his own land. At the time appointed he shall return, and come into the south; but it shall not be in the latter time as it was in the former. For ships of Kittim shall come against him; therefore he shall be grieved, and shall return, and have indignation against the holy covenant, and shall do his pleasure: he shall even return, and have regard unto them that forsake the holy covenant. And arms shall stand on his part, and they shall profane the sanctuary, even the fortress, and shall take away the continual burnt offering, and they shall set up the abomination that maketh desolate. And such as do wickedly against the covenant shall he pervert by flatteries: but the people that know their God shall be strong, and do exploits. And they that be wise among the people shall instruct many: yet they shall fall by the sword and by flame, by captivity and by spoil, many days. Now when they shall

44

fall, they shall be holpen with a little help: but many shall join themselves unto them with flatteries. And some of them that be wise shall fall, to refine them, and to purify, and to make them white, even to the time of the end: because it is yet for the time appointed. And the king shall do according to his will; and he shall exalt himself and magnify himself above every god, and shall speak marvellous things against the God of gods: and he shall prosper till the indignation be accomplished; for that which is determined shall be done. Neither shall he regard the gods of his fathers, nor the desire of women, nor regard any god: for he shall magnify himself above all. But in his place shall he honour the god of fortresses: and a god whom his fathers knew not shall he honour with gold, and silver, and with precious stones, and pleasant things. And he shall deal with the strongest fortresses by the help of a strange god; whosoever acknowledgeth him he will increase with glory: and he shall cause them to rule over many, and shall divide the land for a price. And at the time of the end shall the king of the south contend with him: and the king of the north shall come against him like a whirlwind, with chariots, and with horsemen, and with many ships; and he shall enter into the countries, and shall overflow and pass through. He shall enter also into the glorious land, and many countries shall be overthrown: but these shall be delivered out of his hand, Edom, and Moab, and the chief of the children of Ammon. He shall stretch forth his hand also upon the countries: and the land of Egypt shall not escape. But he shall have power over the treasures of gold and of silver, and over all the precious things of Egypt: and the Libyans and the Ethiopians shall be at his steps. But tidings out of the east and out of the north shall trouble him: and he shall go forth with great fury to destroy and utterly to make away many. And he shall plant the tents of his palace between the sea and the glorious holy mountain; yet he shall come to his end, and none shall help him. And at that time shall Michael stand up, the great prince which standeth for the children of thy people: and there shall be a time of trouble, such as never was since there was a nation even to that same time: and at that time thy people shall be delivered, every one that shall be found written in the book. And many of them that sleep in the dust of the earth shall awake, some to everlasting life, and some to shame and everlasting contempt. And they that be wise shall shine as the brightness of the firmament; and they that turn many to righteousness as the stars for ever and ever. But thou, O Daniel, shut up the words, and seal the book, even to the time of the end: many shall run to and fro, and knowledge shall be increased.

Then I Daniel looked, and, behold, there stood other two, the one on the brink of the river on this side, and the other on the brink of the river on that side. And one said

Daniel 🙰

to the man clothed in linen, which was above the waters of the river, How long shall it be to the end of these wonders? And I heard the man clothed in linen, which was above the waters of the river, when he held up his right hand and his left hand unto heaven, and sware by him that liveth for ever that it shall be for a time, times, and an half; and when they have made an end of breaking in pieces the power of the holy people, all these things shall be finished. And I heard, but I understood not: then said I, O my lord, what shall be the issue of these things? And he said, Go thy way, Daniel: for the words are shut up and sealed till the time of the end. Many shall purify themselves, and make themselves white, and be refined; but the wicked shall do wickedly; and none of the wicked shall understand: but they that be wise shall understand. And from the time that the continual burnt offering shall be taken away, and the abomination that maketh desolate set up, there shall be a thousand two hundred and ninety days. Blessed is he that waiteth and cometh to the thousand three hundred and five and thirty days. But go thou thy way till the end be: for thou shalt rest, and shalt stand in thy lot, at the end of the days.

The Word of the LORD

that came unto

HOSEA

the son of Beeri

in the days of

Uzziah

Jotham

Ahaz

and   Hezekiah

kings of Judah

and in the days of

Jeroboam the son of Joash

king of Israel

HOSEA

i

Gomer: an Emblem

．

When the LORD spake at the first by Hosea, the LORD
said unto Hosea, Go, take unto thee a wife of whoredom
and children of whoredom: for the land doth commit
great whoredom, departing from the LORD. So he went
and took Gomer the daughter of Diblaim; and she conceived, and bare him a son. And the LORD said unto
him, Call his name Jezreel; for yet a little while, and I
will avenge the blood of Jezreel upon the house of Jehu,
and will cause the kingdom of the house of Israel to cease.
And it shall come to pass at that day, that I will break the
bow of Israel in the valley of Jezreel. And she conceived
again, and bare a daughter. And the LORD said unto him,
Call her name 'Lo-ruhamah': for I will 'no more have
mercy' upon the house of Israel, that I should in any wise
pardon them. But I will have mercy upon the house of
Judah, and will save them by the LORD their God, and
will not save them by bow, nor by sword, nor by battle,
by horses, nor by horsemen. Now when she had weaned
Lo-ruhamah, she conceived, and bare a son. And the

Lord said, Call his name 'Lo-ammi': for ye are 'not my people,' and I will not be your God.

Yet the number of the children of Israel shall be as the sand of the sea, which cannot be measured nor numbered; and it shall come to pass that, in the place where it was said unto them, Ye are not my people, it shall be said unto them, Ye are the sons of the living God. And the children of Judah and the children of Israel shall be gathered together, and they shall appoint themselves one head, and shall go up from the land: for great shall be the day of Jezreel. Say ye unto your brethren, Ammi; and to your sisters, Ruhamah.

Plead with your mother, plead; for she is not my wife, neither am I her husband: and let her put away her whoredoms from her face, and her adulteries from between her breasts; lest I strip her naked, and set her as in the day that she was born, and make her as a wilderness, and set her like a dry land, and slay her with thirst; yea, upon her children will I have no mercy; for they be children of whoredom. For their mother hath played the harlot: she that conceived them hath done shamefully: for she said, I will go after my lovers, that give me my bread and my water, my wool and my flax, mine oil and my drink. Therefore, behold, I will hedge up thy way with thorns, and I will make a fence against her, that she shall not find her paths. And she shall follow after her lovers, but she shall not overtake them; and she shall seek them, but shall not

find them : then shall she say, I will go and return to my
first husband ; for then was it better with me than now.
For she did not know that I gave her the corn, and the
wine, and the oil, and multiplied unto her silver and gold,
which they used for Baal.   Therefore will I take back my
corn in the time thereof, and my wine in the season thereof,
and will pluck away my wool and my flax which should have
covered her nakedness.   And now will I discover her lewdness in the sight of her lovers, and none shall deliver her
out of mine hand.   I will also cause all her mirth to cease,
her feasts, her new moons, and her sabbaths, and all her
solemn assemblies.   And I will lay waste her vines and her
fig trees, whereof she hath said, These are my hire that my
lovers have given me : and I will make them a forest, and
the beasts of the field shall eat them.   And I will visit upon
her the days of the Baalim, unto which she burned incense ;
when she decked herself with her earrings and her jewels,
and went after her lovers, and forgat me, saith the LORD.

Therefore, behold, I will allure her, and bring her into
the wilderness, and speak comfortably unto her.   And I
will give her her vineyards from thence, and the valley of
Achor for a door of hope : and she shall make answer
there, as in the days of her youth, and as in the day when
she came up out of the land of Egypt.   And it shall be at
that day, saith the LORD, that thou shalt call me Ishi * ; and
shalt call me no more Baali.*   For I will take away the

* [My husband — my lord.]

53

names of the Baalim out of her mouth, and they shall no more be mentioned by their name. And in that day will I make a covenant for them with the beasts of the field, and with the fowls of heaven, and with the creeping things of the ground: and I will break the bow and the sword and the battle out of the land, and will make them to lie down safely. And I will betroth thee unto me for ever; yea, I will betroth thee unto me in righteousness, and in judgement, and in lovingkindness, and in mercies. I will even betroth thee unto me in faithfulness: and thou shalt know the LORD. And it shall come to pass in that day, I will answer, saith the LORD, I will answer the heavens, and they shall answer the earth; and the earth shall answer the corn, and the wine, and the oil; and they shall answer Jezreel. And I will sow her unto me in the earth; and I will have mercy upon her that had not obtained mercy; and I will say to them which were not my people, Thou art my people; and they shall say, Thou art my God.

2

And the LORD said unto me, Go yet, love a woman beloved of her husband, yet an adulteress, even as the LORD loveth the children of Israel, though they turn unto other gods, and love cakes of raisins. So I bought her to me for fifteen pieces of silver, and an homer of barley, and an half homer of barley: and I said unto her, Thou shalt abide for me many days; thou shalt not play the harlot, and thou shalt not be any man's wife: so will I also be toward thee. For the children of Israel shall abide many days without king, and without prince, and without sacrifice, and without pillar, and without ephod or teraphim: afterward shall the children of Israel return, and seek the LORD their God, and David their king; and shall come with fear unto the LORD and to his goodness in the latter days.

ii

Heavy Corruption and Light Repentance

Hear the word of the LORD, ye children of Israel: for the LORD hath a controversy with the inhabitants of the land, because there is no truth, nor mercy, nor knowledge of God in the land. There is nought but swearing and breaking faith, and killing, and stealing, and committing adultery; they break out, and blood toucheth blood. Therefore shall the land mourn, and every one that dwelleth therein shall languish, with the beasts of the field and the fowls of heaven; yea, the fishes of the sea also shall be taken away.

Yet let no man strive, neither let any man reprove; for thy people are as they that strive with the priest. And thou shalt stumble in the day, and the prophet also shall stumble with thee in the night; and I will destroy thy mother. My people are destroyed for lack of knowledge: because thou hast rejected knowledge, I will also reject thee, that thou shalt be no priest to me: seeing thou hast forgotten the law of thy God, I also will forget thy children. As they were multiplied, so they sinned against me: I will change their glory into shame. They feed on the sin of my people, and set their heart on their iniquity. And it shall be, like people, like priest: and I will punish them for their ways, and will reward them their doings.

And they shall eat, and not have enough; they shall commit whoredom, and shall not increase: because they have left off to take heed to the LORD. Whoredom and wine and new wine take away the understanding. My people ask counsel at their stock, and their staff declareth unto them: for the spirit of whoredom hath caused them to err, and they have gone a whoring from under their God. They sacrifice upon the tops of the mountains, and burn incense upon the hills, under oaks and poplars and terebinths, because the shadow thereof is good; therefore your daughters commit whoredom, and your brides commit adultery. I will not punish your daughters when they commit whoredom, nor your brides when they commit adultery; for they themselves go apart with whores, and they sacrifice with the harlots: and the people that doth not understand shall be overthrown.

Though thou, Israel, play the harlot, yet let not Judah offend; and come not ye unto Gilgal, neither go ye up to

Beth-aven, nor swear, As the LORD liveth. For Israel hath behaved himself stubbornly, like a stubborn heifer: now will the LORD feed them as a lamb in a large place. Ephraim is joined to idols; let him alone. Their carouse is over; they commit whoredom continually; they are given up to love; her rulers are a shame. The wind hath wrapped her up in its wings; and they shall be ashamed because of their sacrifices.

Hear this, O ye priests, and hearken, ye house of Israel, and give ear, O house of the king, for unto you pertaineth the judgement; for ye have been a snare at Mizpah, and a net spread upon Tabor. And the revolters are gone deep in corruption; but I am a rebuker of them all. I know Ephraim, and Israel is not hid from me: for now, O Ephraim, thou hast committed whoredom, Israel is defiled. Their doings will not suffer them to turn unto their God: for the spirit of whoredom is within them, and they know not the LORD. And the pride of Israel doth testify to his face: therefore Israel and Ephraim shall stumble in their iniquity; Judah also shall stumble with them. They shall go with their flocks and with their herds to seek the LORD; but they shall not find him: he hath withdrawn himself from them. They have dealt treacherously against the LORD; for they have borne strange children: now shall the new moon devour them with their fields.

Blow ye the cornet in Gibeah, and the trumpet in Ramah — Sound an alarm at Beth-aven — After thee, Benjamin! —

Ephraim shall become a desolation in the day of rebuke: among the tribes of Israel have I made known that which shall surely be. The princes of Judah are like them that remove the landmark: I will pour out my wrath upon them like water. Ephraim is oppressed, he is crushed in judgement; because he was content to walk after vanity. Therefore am I unto Ephraim as a moth, and to the house of Judah as rottenness. When Ephraim saw his sickness, and Judah saw his wound, then went Ephraim to Assyria, and sent to king Jareb: but he is not able to heal you, neither shall he cure you of your wound. For I will be unto Ephraim as a lion, and as a young lion to the house of Judah: I, even I, will tear and go away; I will carry off, and there shall be none to deliver.

I will go and return to my place, till they acknowledge their offence, and seek my face: in their affliction they will seek me earnestly.

REPENTANT ISRAEL

Come, and let us return unto the LORD: for he hath torn, and he will heal us; he hath smitten, and he will bind us up. After two days will he revive us: on the third day he will raise us up, and we shall live before him. And let us know, let us follow on to know the LORD; his going forth is sure as the morning: and he shall come unto us as the rain, as the latter rain that watereth the earth.

THE LORD

O Ephraim, what shall I do unto thee? O Judah, what shall I do unto thee? for your goodness is as a morning cloud, and as the dew that goeth early away. Therefore have I hewed them by the prophets; I have slain them by the words of my mouth: and thy judgements are as the light that goeth forth. For I desire mercy, and not sacrifice; and the knowledge of God more than burnt offerings. But they are as men that have transgressed a covenant: there have they dealt treacherously against me. Gilead is a city of them that work iniquity, it is stained with blood. And as troops of robbers wait for a man, so the company of priests murder in the way toward Shechem: yea, they have committed lewdness. In the house of Israel I have seen an horrible thing: there whoredom is found in Ephraim, Israel is defiled. Also, O Judah, there is an harvest appointed for thee.

iii

Reaping the Whirlwind

When I bring again the captivity of my people, when I would heal Israel, then is the iniquity of Ephraim discovered, and the wickedness of Samaria; for they commit falsehood: and the thief entereth in, and the troop of robbers spoileth without. And they consider not in their hearts that I remember all their wickedness: now have their own doings beset them about; they are before my face. They make the king glad with their wickedness, and the princes with their lies. They are all adulterers; they are as an oven heated by the baker; he ceaseth to stir the fire, from the kneading of the dough until it be leavened. On 'the day of our king' the princes made themselves sick with the heat of wine; he stretched out his hand with scorners. For they have made ready their heart like an oven, whiles they lie in wait: their baker sleepeth all the night; in the morning it burneth as a flaming fire. They are all hot as an oven, and devour their judges: all their kings are fallen: there is none among them that calleth unto me. Ephraim, he mixeth himself among the peoples; Ephraim is a cake not turned. Strangers have devoured his strength, and he knoweth it not; yea, gray hairs are here and there upon him, and he knoweth it not: and the pride of Israel doth testify to his face.

Yet they have not returned unto the LORD their God, nor sought him, for all this. And Ephraim is like a silly dove, without understanding: they call unto Egypt, they go to Assyria. When they shall go, I will spread my net upon them; I will bring them down as the fowls of the heaven: I will chastise them, as their congregation hath heard. Woe unto them! for they have wandered from me; destruction unto them! for they have trespassed against me: though I would redeem them, yet they have spoken lies against me. And they have not cried unto me with their heart, but they howl upon their beds: they assemble themselves for corn and wine, they rebel against me. Though I have taught and strengthened their arms, yet do they imagine mischief against me. They return, but not to him that is on high; they are like a deceitful bow: their princes shall fall by the sword for the rage of their tongue: this shall be their derision in the land of Egypt.

Set the trumpet to thy mouth: as an eagle he cometh against the house of the LORD; because they have transgressed my covenant, and trespassed against my law. They shall cry unto me, My God, we Israel know thee. Israel hath cast off that which is good: the enemy shall pursue him. They have set up kings, but not by me; they have made princes, and I knew it not: of their silver and their gold have they made them idols, that they may be cut off. He hath cast off thy calf, O Samaria; mine anger is kindled against them: how long will it be ere they attain to innocency? For from Israel is even this; the workman made it, and it is no God: yea, the calf of Samaria shall be broken in pieces. For they sow the wind, and they shall reap the whirlwind.

iv

Sentences

He hath no standing corn; the blade shall yield no meal; if so be it yield, strangers shall swallow it up.

✿

Israel is swallowed up: now are they among the nations as a vessel wherein is no pleasure.

✿

For they are gone up to Assyria, like a wild ass alone by himself.

✿

Ephraim hath hired lovers. Yea, though they hire among the nations, now will I gather them; and they begin to be minished by reason of the burden of the king of princes.

✿

Because Ephraim hath multiplied altars — to sin, altars have been unto him — to sin.

✿

Though I write for him my law in ten thousand precepts, they are counted as a strange thing.

❋

As for the sacrifices of mine offerings, they sacrifice
flesh and eat it; but the LORD accepteth them not: now
will he remember their iniquity, and visit their sins; they
shall return to Egypt.

❋

For Israel hath forgotten his Maker, and builded palaces; and Judah hath multiplied fenced cities: but I will
send a fire upon his cities, and it shall devour the castles
thereof.

V

A Harvest Prophecy

Rejoice not, O Israel, unto exultation, like the peoples;
for thou hast gone a whoring from thy God, thou hast
loved hire upon every cornfloor. The threshing-floor and
the winepress shall not feed them, and the new wine shall
fail her. They shall not dwell in the LORD's land; but
Ephraim shall return to Egypt, and they shall eat unclean
food in Assyria. They shall not pour out wine offerings
to the LORD, neither shall their sacrifices be pleasing unto

him; their bread shall be unto them as the bread of mourners; all that eat thereof shall be polluted: for their bread shall be for their appetite; it shall not come into the house of the LORD. What will ye do in the day of solemn assembly, and in the day of the feast of the LORD? For, lo, they are gone away from destruction: Egypt shall gather them up, Memphis shall bury them; their pleasant things of silver, nettles shall possess them; thorns shall be in their tents.

vi

Sentences of Judgment

The days of visitation are come, the days of recompence are come; Israel shall know it: the prophet is a fool, the man that hath the spirit is mad, for the multitude of thine iniquity, and because the enmity is great.

✿

Ephraim was a watchman with my God: as for the prophet, a fowler's snare is in all his ways, and enmity in the house of his God.

✿

Hosea ⮠

They have deeply corrupted themselves, as in the days
of Gibeah: he will remember their iniquity, he will visit
their sins.

❁

I found Israel like grapes in the wilderness; I saw
your fathers as the firstripe in the fig tree at her first
season: but they came to Baal-peor, and consecrated
themselves unto the shameful thing, and became abominable like that which they loved.

❁

As for Ephraim, their glory shall fly away like a bird.
There shall be no birth, and none with child, and no conception; though they bring up their children, yet will
I bereave them, that there be not a man left. Yea, woe
also to them when I depart from them.

❁

Ephraim, like as I have seen Tyre, is planted in a pleasant place: but Ephraim shall bring out his children to
the slayer.

❁

Give them, O LORD: what wilt thou give? give them
a miscarrying womb and dry breasts.

❁

All their wickedness is in Gilgal; for there I hated them: because of the wickedness of their doings I will drive them out of mine house: I will love them no more; all their princes are revolters.

❋

Ephraim is smitten, their root is dried up, they shall bear no fruit: yea, though they bring forth, yet will I slay the beloved fruit of their womb. My God will cast them away, because they did not hearken unto him: and they shall be wanderers among the nations.

❋

Israel is a luxuriant vine, which putteth forth his fruit: according to the multitude of his fruit he hath multiplied his altars; according to the goodness of his land they have made goodly pillars. Their heart is smooth; now shall they be found guilty: he shall smite their altars, he shall spoil their pillars.

❋

Surely now shall they say, We have no king: for we fear not the LORD; and the king, what can he do for us?

❋

They speak vain words, swearing falsely in making covenants: therefore judgement springeth up as hemlock in the furrows of the field.

❋

Hosea &

The inhabitants of Samaria shall be in terror for the calves of Beth-aven : for the people thereof shall mourn over it, and the priests thereof that rejoiced over it, for the glory thereof, because it is departed from it. It also shall be carried unto Assyria for a present to king Jareb : Ephraim shall receive shame, and Israel shall be ashamed of his own counsel.

&

Samaria is cut off with her king, as foam upon the water. The high places also of Aven, the sin of Israel, shall be destroyed : the thorn and the thistle shall come up on their altars. And they shall say to the mountains, Cover us ; and to the hills, Fall on us.

&

O Israel, thou hast sinned from the days of Gibeah : there they stood ; shall not the battle against the children of iniquity overtake them in Gibeah?

&

When it is my desire, I will chastise them ; and the peoples shall be gathered against them, when they are yoked to their two transgressions.

&

And Ephraim is an heifer that is taught, that loveth to tread out the corn ; but I have passed over upon her fair neck: I will set a rider on Ephraim; Judah shall plow, Jacob shall break his clods.

❀

Sow to yourselves in righteousness, reap according to mercy; break up your fallow ground: for it is time to seek the LORD, till he come and rain righteousness upon you.

❀

Ye have plowed wickedness, ye have reaped iniquity; ye have eaten the fruit of lies: for thou didst trust in thy way, in the multitude of thy mighty men. Therefore shall a tumult arise among thy people, and all thy fortresses shall be spoiled, as Shalman spoiled Beth-arbel in the day of battle: the mother was dashed in pieces with her children. So shall it be done unto you at Beth-el because of your great wickedness: at daybreak shall the king of Israel be utterly cut off.

vii

The Yearning of God

THE LORD

When Israel was a child, then I loved him, and called my son out of Egypt. —
As they called them, so they went from them: they

sacrificed unto the Baalim, and burned incense to graven
images. —

Yet I taught Ephraim to go; I took them on my arms;
but they knew not that I healed them. I drew them with
cords of a man, with bands of love; and I was to them as
they that take off the yoke on their jaws, and I laid meat
before them. —

He shall not return into the land of Egypt; but the
Assyrian shall be his king, because they refused to return.
And the sword shall fall upon his cities, and shall consume his bars, and devour them, because of their own
counsels. And my people are bent to backsliding from
me: though they call them to him that is on high, none
at all will lift himself up. —

How shall I give thee up, Ephraim? how shall I deliver
thee, Israel? how shall I make thee as Admah? how
shall I set thee as Zeboim? mine heart is turned within
me, my compassions are kindled together. I will not
execute the fierceness of mine anger, I will not return
to destroy Ephraim: for I am God, and not man; the
Holy One in the midst of thee: and I will not come in
wrath. They shall walk after the LORD, who shall roar
like a lion: for he shall roar, and the children shall come
trembling from the west. They shall come trembling as
a bird out of Egypt, and as a dove out of the land of
Assyria: and I will make them to dwell in their houses,
saith the LORD. —

Ephraim compasseth me about with falsehood, and the
house of Israel with deceit: and Judah is yet unsteadfast
with God, and with the Holy One who is faithful.
Ephraim feedeth on wind, and followeth after the east
wind: he continually multiplieth lies and desolation; and
they make a covenant with Assyria, and oil is carried
into Egypt. The LORD hath also a controversy with
Judah, and will punish Jacob according to his ways;
according to his doings will he recompense him. —

'In the womb he took his brother by the heel;
   And in his manhood he had power with God:
Yea, he had power over the angel, and prevailed,
   He wept, and made supplication unto him.
He found him at Beth-el, and there he spake with us;
   Even the LORD, the God of hosts, the LORD is his
     memorial.'

Therefore turn thou to thy God: keep mercy and judgement, and wait on thy God continually. —

He is a trafficker, the balances of deceit are in his hand:
he loveth to oppress. And Ephraim said, Surely I am
become rich, I have found me wealth: in all my labours
they shall find in me none iniquity that were sin. But I am
the LORD thy God from the land of Egypt; I will yet
again make thee to dwell in tents, as in the days of the
solemn feast. I have also spoken unto the prophets, and

I have multiplied visions; and by the ministry of the prophets have I used similitudes. Is Gilead iniquity? they are altogether vanity; in 'Gilgal' they sacrifice bullocks: yea, their altars are as 'heaps' in the furrows of the field. —

> 'And Jacob fled into the field of Aram,
>> And Israel served for a wife, and for a wife he kept sheep.
>
> And by a prophet the LORD brought Israel up out of Egypt,
> And by a prophet was he preserved.' —

Ephraim hath provoked to anger most bitterly: therefore shall his blood be left upon him, and his reproach shall his Lord return unto him. When Ephraim spake with trembling he exalted himself in Israel: but when he offended in Baal, he died. And now they sin more and more, and have made them molten images of their silver, even idols according to their own understanding, all of them the work of the craftsmen: they say of them, Let the men that sacrifice kiss the calves. Therefore they shall be as the morning cloud, and as the dew that passeth early away, as the chaff that is driven with the whirlwind out of the threshing-floor, and as the smoke out of the chimney. —

Yet I am the LORD thy God from the land of Egypt;

and thou knowest no god but me, and beside me there
is no saviour. I did know thee in the wilderness, in the
land of great drought. According to their pasture, so were
they filled; they were filled, and their heart was exalted:
therefore have they forgotten me. —

Therefore am I unto them as a lion: as a leopard will
I watch by the way: I will meet them as a bear that is
bereaved of her whelps, and will rend the caul of their
heart: and there will I devour them like a lion; the wild
beast shall tear them. It is thy destruction, O Israel,
that thou art against me, against thy help. Where now
is thy king, that he may save thee in all thy cities?
and thy judges, of whom thou saidst, Give me a king and
princes? I have given thee a king in mine anger, and
have taken him away in my wrath. The iniquity of
Ephraim is bound up; his sin is laid up in store. The
sorrows of a travailing woman shall come upon him: he is
an unwise son; when it is time, he standeth not in the
place of the breaking forth of children. —

I will ransom them from the power of the grave; I will
redeem them from death: O death, where are thy plagues?
O grave, where is thy destruction? —

Repentance shall be hid from mine eyes. Though he
be fruitful among his brethren, an east wind shall come,
the breath of the LORD coming up from the wilderness,
and his spring shall become dry, and his fountain shall be
dried up: it shall spoil the treasure of all pleasant vessels.

Samaria shall bear her guilt; for she hath rebelled against her God: they shall fall by the sword; their infants shall be dashed in pieces, and their women with child shall be ripped up.

REPENTANT ISRAEL

O Israel, return unto the LORD thy God; for thou hast fallen by thine iniquity. Take with you words, and return unto the LORD: say unto him, Take away all iniquity, and accept that which is good: so will we render as bullocks the offering of our lips. Asshur shall not save us; we will not ride upon horses: neither will we say any more to the work of our hands, Ye are our Gods: for in thee the fatherless findeth mercy.

THE LORD

I will heal their backsliding, I will love them freely: for mine anger is turned away from him. I will be as the dew unto Israel: he shall blossom as the lily, and cast forth his roots as Lebanon. His branches shall spread, and his beauty shall be as the olive tree, and his smell as Lebanon. They that dwell under his shadow shall return; they shall revive as the corn, and blossom as the vine: the scent thereof shall be as the wine of Lebanon.

EPHRAIM

What have I to do any more with idols?

73

THE LORD

I have answered, and will regard him.

EPHRAIM

I am like a green fir tree —

THE LORD

From me is thy fruit found.

* *
*

Who is wise, and he shall understand these things?
Prudent, and he shall know them?
For the ways of the Lord are right,
And the just shall walk in them:
But transgressors shall fall therein.

The Word of the LORD

that came to

JOEL

the son of Pethuel

JOEL

A RHAPSODY OF THE LOCUST PLAGUE

i

The Land Desolate and Mourning

OLD MEN

Hear this, ye old men,
And give ear, all ye inhabitants of the land!
Hath this been in your days,
Or in the days of your fathers?
Tell ye your children of it,
And let your children tell their children,
And their children another generation.
That which the palmerworm hath left
Hath the locust eaten;
And that which the locust hath left
Hath the cankerworm eaten;
And that which the cankerworm hath left
Hath the caterpillar eaten.

REVELLERS

Awake, ye drunkards, and weep,
And howl, all ye drinkers of wine,

77

Because of the sweet wine;
For it is cut off from your mouth!
For a nation is come up upon my land,
Strong, and without number;
His teeth are the teeth of a lion,
And he hath the jaw teeth of a great lion.
He hath laid my vine waste,
And barked my fig tree :
He hath made it clean bare, and cast it away;
The branches thereof are made white.

PRIESTS

Lament like a virgin
Girded with sackcloth for the husband of her youth!
The meal offering and the drink offering
Is cut off from the house of the LORD :
The priests, the LORD'S ministers, mourn.
The field is wasted,
The land mourneth;
For the corn is wasted,
The new wine is dried up,
The oil languisheth.

HUSBANDMEN

Be ashamed, O ye husbandmen,
Howl, O ye vinedressers,
For the wheat, and for the barley;

Joel ✂

For the harvest of the field is perished!
The wine is withered,
And the fig tree languisheth;
The pomegranate tree,
The palm tree also, and the apple tree,
Even all the trees of the field are withered:
For joy is withered away from the sons of men.

PRIESTS

Gird yourselves, and lament, ye priests;
Howl, ye ministers of the altar;
Come, lie all night in sackcloth,
Ye ministers of my God:
For the meal offering and the drink offering
Is withholden from the house of your God!

THE WHOLE PEOPLE

Sanctify a fast, call a solemn assembly, gather the old
men and all the inhabitants of the land unto the house of
the LORD your God, and cry unto the LORD:

Alas for the day! for the day of the LORD is at hand!
And as destruction from the Almighty shall it
come.
Is not the meat cut off before our eyes,
Yea, joy and gladness from the house of our God?

The seeds rot under their clods:
  The garners are laid desolate,
  The barns are broken down;
  For the corn is withered.

How do the beasts groan!
  The herds of cattle are perplexed,
  Because they have no pasture;
  Yea, the flocks of sheep are made desolate.

O Lord, to thee do I cry:
  For the fire hath devoured the pastures of the
    wilderness,
  And the flame hath burned all the trees of the field.
Yea, the beasts of the field pant unto thee:
  For the water brooks are dried up,
  And the fire hath devoured the pastures of the
    wilderness.

ii

The Judgment Advancing

Blow ye the trumpet in Zion,
And sound an alarm in my holy mountain;
Let all the inhabitants of the land tremble!

Joel &

For the Day of the LORD cometh, for it is nigh at hand;
a day of darkness and gloominess, a day of clouds and
thick darkness, as the dawn spread upon the mountains;
a great people and a strong, there hath not been ever the
like, neither shall be any more after them, even to the
years of many generations!

> A fire devoureth before them;
> And behind them a flame burneth ::
> The land is as the garden of Eden before them,
> And behind them a desolate wilderness!

Yea, and none hath escaped them. The appearance of
them is as the appearance of horses; and as horsemen, so
do they run. Like the noise of chariots on the tops of the
mountains do they leap, like the noise of a flame of fire
that devoureth the stubble, as a strong people set in battle
array.

> At their presence the peoples are in anguish:
> All faces are waxed pale:
> They run like mighty men;
> They climb the wall like men of war;
> And they march every one on his ways.

And they break not their ranks: neither doth one thrust
another; they march every one in his path: and they
burst through the weapons, and break not off their course.

They leap upon the city;
They run upon the wall;
They climb up into the houses;
They enter in at the windows like a thief.
The earth quaketh before them;
The heavens tremble:
The sun and the moon are darkened,
And the stars withdraw their shining.

And the LORD uttereth his voice before his army; for his camp is very great; for he is strong that executeth his word: for the Day of the LORD is great and very terrible; and who can abide it?

iii

Repentance at the Last Moment

THE LORD

Yet even now, saith the LORD, turn ye unto me with all your heart, and with fasting, and with weeping, and with mourning: and rend your heart, and not your garments, and turn unto the LORD your God: for he is gracious and full of compassion, slow to anger, and plenteous in mercy, and repenteth him of the evil.

Joel ✌

The People

Who knoweth whether he will not turn and repent, and leave a blessing behind him, even a meal offering and a drink offering unto the LORD your God?

> Blow the trumpet in Zion,
> Sanctify a fast,
> Call a solemn assembly:
> Gather the people,
> Sanctify the congregation,
> Assemble the old men,
> Gather the children, and those that suck the breasts:
> Let the bridegroom go forth of his chamber,
> And the bride out of her closet.

Let the priests, the ministers of the LORD, weep between the porch and the altar, and let them say:

Priests

> Spare thy people, O LORD,
> And give not thine heritage to reproach,
> That the nations should use a byword against them,
> Wherefore should they say among the peoples,
> Where is their God?

iv

Relief and Restoration

Then was the LORD jealous for his land, and had pity on his people.

THE LORD

Behold, I will send you corn, and wine, and oil, and ye shall be satisfied therewith: and I will no more make you a reproach among the nations: but I will remove far off from you the northern army, and will drive him into a land barren and desolate, his forepart into the eastern sea, and his hinder part into the western sea; and his stink shall come up, and his ill savour shall come up, because he hath done great things.

Fear not, O land, be glad and rejoice; for the LORD hath done great things. Be not afraid, ye beasts of the field; for the pastures of the wilderness do spring, for the tree beareth her fruit, the fig tree and the vine do yield their strength. Be glad then, ye children of Zion, and rejoice in the LORD your God: for he giveth you the former rain in just measure, and he causeth to come down for you the rain, the former rain and the latter rain, in the first month. And the floors shall be full of wheat, and the fats shall overflow with wine and oil. And I will restore to you the years that the locust hath eaten, the canker-worm, and the caterpiller, and the palmerworm, my great army which I sent among you. And ye shall eat in plenty and be satisfied, and shall praise the name of the LORD your God, that hath dealt wondrously with you : and my people shall never be ashamed. And ye shall know that I am in the midst of Israel, and that I am the LORD your God, and there is none else : and my people shall never be ashamed.

V

Afterward

THE LORD

And it shall come to pass afterward, that I will pour out my spirit upon all flesh ; and your sons and your daughters shall prophesy, your old men shall dream dreams, your young men shall see visions : and also upon the servants and upon the handmaids in those days will I pour out my spirit.

And I will shew wonders in the heavens and in the earth, blood, and fire, and pillars of smoke. The sun shall be turned into darkness, and the moon into blood, before the great and terrible day of the LORD come. And it shall come to pass, that whosoever shall call on the name of the

LORD shall be delivered : for in mount Zion and in Jerusalem there shall be those that escape; as the LORD hath
said, and in the remnant whom the LORD doth call. For,
behold, in those days, and in that time, when I shall bring
again the captivity of Judah and Jerusalem, I will gather
all nations, and will bring them down into the Valley
of Jehoshaphat * ; and I will plead with them there for
my people and for my heritage Israel, whom they have
scattered among the nations, and parted my land. And
they have cast lots for my people : and have given a boy
for an harlot, and sold a girl for wine, that they might drink.
Yea, and what are ye to me, O Tyre, and Zidon, and all
the regions of Philistia? will ye render me a recompence?
and if ye recompense me, swiftly and speedily will I return
your recompence upon your own head. Forasmuch as ye
have taken my silver and my gold, and have carried into
your temples my goodly pleasant things ; the children also
of Judah and the children of Jerusalem have ye sold unto
the sons of the Grecians, that ye might remove them far
from their border : behold, I will stir them up out of the
place whither ye have sold them, and will return your
recompence upon your own head; and I will sell your sons
and your daughters into the hand of the children of Judah,
and they shall sell them to the men of Sheba, to a nation
far off : for the LORD hath spoken it.

* [The LORD's Decision.]

86

vi

Advance to the Valley of Decision

THE LORD

Proclaim ye this among the nations; prepare war: stir up the mighty men; let all the men of war draw near, let them come up. Beat your plowshares into swords, and your pruninghooks into spears: let the weak say, I am strong.

VOICES

Haste ye, and come, all ye nations round about, and gather yourselves together. Thither cause thy mighty ones to come down, O LORD.

THE LORD

Let the nations bestir themselves. and come up to the Valley of 'Jehoshaphat': for there will I 'sit to judge' all the nations round about.

THE LORD (*to his Hosts*)

Put ye in the sickle, for the harvest is ripe: come, tread ye; for the winepress is full, the fats overflow; for their wickedness is great.

The Prophetic Spectator

Multitudes, multitudes in the Valley of Decision! for the Day of the LORD is near in the Valley of Decision. The sun and the moon are darkened, and the stars withdraw their shining. And the LORD shall roar from Zion, and utter his voice from Jerusalem; and the heavens and the earth shall shake: but the LORD will be a refuge unto his people, and a strong hold to the children of Israel.

vii

The Holy Mountain and Eternal Peace

The Lord

So shall ye know that I am the LORD your God, dwelling in Zion my holy mountain: then shall Jerusalem be holy, and there shall no strangers pass through her any more. And it shall come to pass in that day, that the mountains shall drop down sweet wine, and the hills shall flow with milk, and all the brooks of Judah shall flow with waters; and a fountain shall come forth of the house of the LORD, and shall water the Valley of Acacias. Egypt shall be a desolation, and Edom shall be a desolate wilderness, for the violence done to the children of Judah, be-

Joel 〰

cause they have shed innocent blood in their land. But Judah shall be inhabited for ever, and Jerusalem from generation to generation. And I will cleanse their blood that I have not cleansed: for the LORD dwelleth in Zion.

THE BOOK

OF

AMOS

AMOS

AN ORACLE OF THE EARTHQUAKE

A RHAPSODY OF THE JUDGMENT TO COME

AN ORACLE OF THE EARTHQUAKE

The words of Amos, who was among the herdmen of Tekoa, which he saw concerning Israel in the days of Uzziah king of Judah, and in the days of Jeroboam the son of Joash king of Israel, two years before the Earthquake. And he said:

The LORD shall roar from Zion,
   And utter his voice from Jerusalem:
And the habitations of the shepherds shall mourn,
   And the top of Carmel shall wither.

A RHAPSODY OF

THE JUDGMENT TO COME

i

Israel among the Doomed Nations

Thus saith the LORD:
    For three transgressions of Damascus,
    Yea, for four,
I will not turn away the punishment thereof;

because they have threshed Gilead with threshing instruments of iron:

    But I will send a fire into the house of Hazael
    And it shall devour the palaces of Ben-hadad.

And I will break the bar of Damascus, and cut off the inhabitant from the valley of Aven, and him that holdeth the sceptre from the house of Eden: and the people of Syria shall go into captivity unto Kir, saith the LORD.

2

Thus saith the LORD:
    For three transgressions of Gaza,
    Yea, for four,
I will not turn away the punishment thereof;

because they carried away captive the whole people, to deliver them up to Edom:

    But I will send a fire on the wall of Gaza,
    And it shall devour the palaces thereof:

and I will cut off the inhabitant from Ashdod, and him that holdeth the sceptre from Ashkelon; and I will turn mine hand against Ekron, and the remnant of the Philistines shall perish, saith the Lord GOD.

Thus saith the LORD:
    For three transgressions of Tyre,
    Yea, for four,
I will not turn away the punishment thereof;

because they delivered up the whole people to Edom, and remembered not the brotherly covenant:

    But I will send a fire on the wall of Tyre,
    And it shall devour the palaces thereof.

Thus saith the LORD:
>
> For three transgressions of Edom,
> Yea, for four,
I will not turn away the punishment thereof;

because he did pursue his brother with the sword, and did cast off all pity, and his anger did tear perpetually, and he kept his wrath for ever:

> But I will send a fire upon Teman,
> And it shall devour the palaces of Bozrah.

Thus saith the LORD:
>
> For three transgressions of the children of Ammon,
> Yea, for four,
I will not turn away the punishment thereof;

because they have ripped up the women with child of Gilead, that they might enlarge their border:

> But I will kindle a fire in the wall of Rabbah,
> And it shall devour the palaces thereof,

with shouting in the day of battle, with a tempest in the day of the whirlwind: and their king shall go into captivity, he and his princes together, saith the LORD.

96

Thus saith the LORD:
　For three transgressions of Moab,
　Yea, for four,
I will not turn away the punishment thereof;

because he burned the bones of the king of Edom into lime:
　But I will send a fire upon Moab,
　And it shall devour the palaces of Kerioth;

and Moab shall die with tumult, with shouting, and with the sound of the trumpet; and I will cut off the judge from the midst thereof, and will slay all the princes thereof with him, saith the LORD.

Thus saith the LORD:
　For three transgressions of Judah,
　Yea, for four,
I will not turn away the punishment thereof;

because they have rejected the law of the LORD, and have not kept his statutes, and their lies have caused them to err, after the which their fathers did walk:

　But I will send a fire upon Judah,
　And it shall devour the palaces of Jerusalem.

Thus saith the LORD:
    For three transgressions of Israel,
    Yea, for four,
    I will not turn away the punishment thereof;

because they have sold the righteous for silver, and the
needy for a pair of shoes: that pant after the dust of the
earth on the head of the poor, and turn aside the way of
the meek: and a man and his father will go unto the same
maid, to profane my holy name: and they lay themselves
down beside every altar upon clothes taken in pledge, and
in the house of their God they drink the wine of such as
have been fined. Yet destroyed I the Amorite before
them, whose height was like the height of the cedars, and
he was strong as the oaks; yet I destroyed his fruit from
above, and his roots from beneath. Also I brought you
up out of the land of Egypt, and led you forty years in the
wilderness, to possess the land of the Amorite. And I
raised up of your sons for prophets, and of your young
men for Nazirites. Is it not even thus, O ye children of
Israel? saith the LORD. But ye gave the Nazirites wine
to drink; and commanded the prophets, saying, Prophesy
not.

Behold I will press you in your place,
As a cart presseth that is full of sheaves.
And flight shall perish from the swift,

And the strong shall not strengthen his force,
Neither shall the mighty deliver himself:
Neither shall he stand that handleth the bow;
And he that is swift of foot shall not deliver himself:
Neither shall he that rideth the horse deliver himself:
And he that is courageous among the mighty
Shall flee away naked in that day, saith the LORD.

ii

Corruption ripe for Judgment

Hear this word that the LORD hath spoken against you,
O children of Israel, against the whole family which I
brought up out of the land of Egypt, saying, You only
have I known of all the families of the earth: therefore
I will visit upon you all your iniquities.

*(Shall two walk together except they have agreed?
Will a lion roar in the forest, when he hath no prey?
will a young lion cry out of his den, if he have taken
nothing? Can a bird fall in a snare upon the earth,
where no gin is set for him? shall a snare spring up
from the ground, and have taken nothing at all?
Shall the trumpet be blown in a city, and the people
not be afraid? Shall evil befall a city, and the LORD
hath not done it? Surely the Lord GOD will do noth-*

99

ing, but he revealeth his secret unto his servants the prophets. The lion hath roared, who will not fear? the Lord GOD hath spoken, who can but prophesy?)

Publish ye in the palaces at Ashdod, and in the palaces in the land of Egypt, and say, Assemble yourselves upon the mountains of Samaria, and behold what great tumults are therein, and what oppressions in the midst thereof. For they know not to do right, saith the LORD, who store up violence and robbery in their palaces. Therefore thus saith the Lord GOD: An adversary there shall be, even round about the land: and he shall bring down thy strength from thee, and thy palaces shall be spoiled. Thus saith the LORD: As the shepherd rescueth out of the mouth of the lion two legs, or a piece of an ear; so shall the children of Israel be rescued that sit in Samaria in the corner of a couch, and on the silken cushions of a bed.

Hear ye, and testify against the house of Jacob, saith the Lord GOD, the God of hosts. For in the day that I shall visit the transgressions of Israel upon him, I will also visit the altars of Beth-el, and the horns of the altar shall be cut off, and fall to the ground. And I will smite the winter house with the summer house; and the houses of ivory shall perish, and the great houses shall have an end, saith the LORD.

3

Hear this word, ye kine of Bashan, that are in the mountains of Samaria, which oppress the poor, which crush the needy, which say unto their lords, Bring, and let us drink. The Lord GOD hath sworn by his holiness, that, lo, the days shall come upon you, that they shall take you away with hooks, and your residue with fish hooks. And ye shall go out at the breaches, every one straight before her; and ye shall cast yourselves into Harmon, saith the LORD.

(Come to Bethel—and transgress; to Gilgal—and multiply transgression; and bring your sacrifices every morning, and your tithes every three days; and offer a sacrifice of thanksgiving of that which is leavened, and proclaim freewill offerings and publish them:

For this liketh you, O ye children of Israel,
Saith the Lord GOD.

And I also have given you cleanness of teeth in all your cities, and want of bread in all your places:

Yet have ye not returned unto me,
Saith the LORD.

And I also have withholden the rain from you, when there were yet three months to the harvest: and I caused it to rain upon one city, and caused it not to rain upon another city: one piece was rained upon, and the piece whereupon it rained not withered. So two or three cities wandered unto one city to drink water, and were not satisfied:

> *Yet have ye not returned unto me,*
> *Saith the LORD.*

I have smitten you with blasting and mildew: the multitude of your gardens and your vineyards and your fig trees and your olive trees hath the palmer-worm devoured:

> *Yet have ye not returned unto me,*
> *Saith the LORD.*

I have sent among you the pestilence after the manner of Egypt: your young men have I slain with the sword, and have carried away your horses; and I have made the stink of your camp to come up, even into your nostrils:

> *Yet have ye not returned unto me,*
> *Saith the LORD.*

Amos &

I have overturned some among you, as when God overthrew Sodom and Gomorrah, and ye were as a brand plucked out of the burning :

> *Yet have ye not returned unto me,*
> *Saith the LORD.*

Therefore THUS will I do unto thee, O Israel :

> *And because I will do THIS unto thee,*
> *Prepare to meet thy God, O Israel.*

For, lo, he that formeth the mountains, and createth the wind, and declareth unto man what is his thought, that maketh the morning darkness, and treadeth upon the high places of the earth ; the LORD, the God of hosts, is his name.)

4

Hear ye this word which I take up for a lamentation over you, O house of Israel.

> The virgin of Israel is fallen — she shall no more rise!
> She is cast down upon her land — there is none to raise
>   her up!

For thus saith the Lord GOD : The city that went forth a thousand shall have an hundred left, and that which went forth an hundred shall have ten left, to the house of Israel. For thus saith the LORD unto the house of Israel: Seek ye me, and ye shall live: but seek not Beth-el, nor enter into Gilgal, and pass not to Beer-sheba: for Gilgal shall surely go into captivity, and Beth-el shall come to nought. Seek the LORD, and ye shall live; lest he break out like fire in the house of Joseph, and it devour and there be none to quench it in Beth-el: ye who turn judgement to wormwood, and cast down righteousness to the earth. Seek him that maketh the Pleiades and Orion, and turneth the shadow of death into the morning, and maketh the day dark with night; that calleth for the waters of the sea, and poureth them out upon the face of the earth — the LORD is his name — that bringeth sudden destruction upon the strong, so that destruction cometh upon the fortress.

(They hate him that reproveth in the gate, and they abhor him that speaketh uprightly.)

Forasmuch therefore as ye trample upon the poor, and take exactions from him of wheat: ye have built houses of hewn stone, but ye shall not dwell in them; ye have planted pleasant vineyards, but ye shall not drink the wine thereof. For I know how manifold are your transgressions and how mighty are your sins; ye that afflict the just, that take a bribe, and that turn aside the needy in the gate from their right.

Amos ✂

('Therefore he that is prudent shall keep silence in such a time; for it is an evil time.')

Seek good, and not evil, that ye may live: and so the LORD, the God of hosts, shall be with you, as ye say. Hate the evil, and love the good, and establish judgement in the gate.

('It may be that the LORD, the God of hosts, will be gracious unto the remnant of Joseph.')

Therefore thus saith the LORD, the God of hosts, the Lord: Wailing shall be in all the broad ways; and they shall say in all the streets, Alas! alas! and they shall call the husbandman to mourning, and such as are skilful of lamentation to wailing. And in all vineyards shall be wailing: for I will pass through the midst of thee, saith the LORD.

Woe unto you that desire the day of the LORD. Wherefore would ye have the day of the LORD? it is darkness, and not light. As if a man did flee from a lion, and a bear met him; or went into the house and leaned his hand on the wall, and a serpent bit him. Shall not the day of the LORD be darkness, and not light? even very dark, and no brightness in it? I hate, I despise your feasts, and I will take no delight in your solemn as-

semblies. Yea, though ye offer me your burnt offerings
and meal offerings, I will not accept them: neither will I
regard the peace'offerings of your fat beasts. Take thou
away from me the noise of thy songs; for I will not hear
the melody of thy viols. But let judgement roll down as
waters, and righteousness as a mighty stream. Did ye
bring unto me sacrifices and offerings in the wilderness
forty years, O house of Israel? Yea, ye shall take up the
tabernacle of your king and the shrine of your images, the
star of your god, which ye made to yourselves; and I
will cause you to go into captivity beyond Damascus,
saith the LORD, whose name is the God of hosts.

6

Woe to them that are at ease in Zion, and to them that
are secure in the mountain of Samaria, the notable men of
the chief of the nations, to whom the house of Israel
come! Pass ye unto Calneh, and see; and from thence
go ye to Hamath the great: then go down to Gath of the
Philistines: be they better than these kingdoms? or is
their border greater than your border? Ye that put far
away the evil day, and cause the seat of violence to come
near; that lie upon beds of ivory, and stretch themselves
upon their couches, and eat the lambs out of the flock,
and the calves out of the midst of the stall; that sing idle
songs to the sound of the viol; that devise for themselves
instruments of music, like David; that drink wine in

bowls, and anoint themselves with the chief ointments; but they are not grieved for the affliction of Joseph. Therefore now shall they go captive with the first that go captive, and the revelry of them that stretched themselves shall pass away.

7

The Lord GOD hath sworn by himself, saith the LORD, the God of hosts: I abhor the excellency of Jacob, and hate his palaces: therefore will I deliver up the city with all that is therein. And it shall come to pass, if there remain ten men in one house, that they shall die. And when a man's kinsman shall take him up, even he that burneth him, to bring out the bones out of the house, and shall say unto him that is in the innermost parts of the house, Is there yet any with thee? and he shall say, No; then shall he say, Hold thy peace; for we may not make mention of the name of the LORD. For, behold, the LORD commandeth, and the great house shall be smitten with breaches, and the little house with clefts. Shall horses run upon the rock? will one plow there with oxen? that ye have turned judgement into gall, and the fruit of righteousness into wormwood: ye which rejoice in a thing of nought, which say, Have we not taken to us horns by our own strength? For, behold, I will raise up against you a nation, O house of Israel, saith the LORD, the God of hosts; and they shall afflict you from the entering in of Hamath unto the brook of the Arabah.

iii

Vision of Judgment

1

Thus the Lord GOD shewed me: and, behold, he formed locusts in the beginning of the shooting up of the latter growth; and, lo, it was the latter growth after the king's mowings. And it came to pass that when they made an end of eating the grass of the land, then I said, O Lord GOD, forgive, I beseech thee: how shall Jacob stand? for he is small. The LORD repented concerning this: It shall not be, saith the LORD.

2

Thus the Lord GOD shewed me: and, behold, the Lord GOD called to contend by fire; and it devoured the great deep, and would have eaten up the land. Then said I, O Lord GOD, cease, I beseech thee: how shall Jacob stand? for he is small. The LORD repented concerning this: This also shall not be, saith the Lord GOD.

3

Thus he shewed me: and, behold, the Lord stood beside a wall made by a plumbline, with a plumbline in his hand. And the LORD said unto me, Amos, what seest

103

thou? And I said, A plumbline. Then said the Lord, Behold, I will set a plumbline in the midst of my people Israel; I will not again pass by them any more: and the high places of Isaac shall be desolate, and the sanctuaries of Israel shall be laid waste; and I will rise against the house of Jeroboam with the sword.

(Then Amaziah the priest of Beth-el sent to Jeroboam king of Israel, saying, Amos hath conspired against thee in the midst of the house of Israel: the land is not able to bear all his words. For thus Amos saith, Jeroboam shall die by the sword, and Israel shall surely be led away captive out of his land. Also Amaziah said unto Amos, O thou seer, go, flee thee away into the land of Judah, and there eat bread, and prophesy there: but prophesy not again any more at Beth-el: for it is the king's sanctuary, and it is a royal house. Then answered Amos, and said to Amaziah, I was no prophet, neither was I a prophet's son; but I was an herdman, and a dresser of sycomore trees: and the LORD took me from following the flock, and the LORD said unto me, Go, prophesy unto my people Israel. Now therefore hear thou the word of the LORD: Thou sayest, Prophesy not against Israel, and drop not thy word against the house of Isaac; therefore thus saith the LORD: Thy wife shall be an harlot in the city, and thy sons and thy daughters

*shall fall by the sword, and thy land shall be divided
by line; and thou thyself shalt die in a land that is
unclean, and Israel shall surely be led away captive out
of his land.)*

4

Thus the Lord GOD shewed me: and behold, a basket of
summer fruit. And he said, Amos, what seest thou? And
I said, A basket of summer fruit. Then said the LORD
unto me, The end is come upon my people Israel; I will
not again pass by them any more. And the songs of the
temple shall be howlings in that day, saith the Lord GOD:
the dead bodies shall be many; in every place shall they
cast them forth with silence.

*(Hear this, O ye that would swallow up the needy,
and cause the poor of the land to fail, saying, When
will the new moon be gone, that we may sell corn? and
the sabbath, that we may set forth wheat? making the
ephah small, and the shekel great, and dealing falsely
with balances of deceit; that we may buy the poor for
silver, and the needy for a pair of shoes, and sell the
refuse of the wheat. The LORD hath sworn by the
excellency of Jacob, Surely I will never forget any of
their works. Shall not the land tremble for this, and
every one mourn that dwelleth therein? yea, it shall
rise up wholly like the River; and it shall be troubled
and sink again, like the River of Egypt.)*

Amos ⅛←

And it shall come to pass in that day, saith the Lord
GOD, that I will cause the sun to go down at noon, and I
will darken the earth in the clear day. And I will turn
your feasts into mourning, and all your songs into lamentation; and I will bring up sackcloth upon all loins, and
baldness upon every head; and I will make it as the
mourning for an only son, and the end thereof as a bitter
day. Behold, the days come, saith the Lord GOD, that I
will send a famine in the land, not a famine of bread, nor
a thirst for water, but of hearing the words of the LORD.
And they shall wander from sea to sea, and from the north
even to the east; they shall run to and fro to seek the word
of the LORD, and shall not find it. In that day shall the
fair virgins and the young men faint for thirst. They that
swear by the sin of Samaria, and say, As thy God, O Dan,
liveth; and, As the way of Beer-Sheba liveth; even they
shall fall, and never rise up again.

9

I saw the Lord standing beside the altar: and he said,
Smite the chapiters, that the thresholds may shake: and
break them in pieces on the head of all of them; and I
will slay the last of them with the sword: there shall not
one of them flee away, and there shall not one of them
escape. Though they dig into hell, thence shall mine hand
take them; and though they climb up to heaven, thence
will I bring them down. And though they hide them-

selves in the top of Carmel, I will search and take them out thence; and though they be hid from my sight in the bottom of the sea, thence will I command the serpent, and he shall bite them. And though they go into captivity before their enemies, thence will I command the sword, and it shall slay them: and I will set mine eyes upon them for evil, and not for good.

(For the Lord, the GOD of hosts, is he that toucheth the land and it melteth, and all that dwell therein shall mourn; and it shall rise up wholly like the River; and shall sink again, like the River of Egypt; it is he that buildeth his chambers in the heaven, and hath founded his vault upon the earth; he that calleth for the waters of the sea and poureth them out upon the face of the earth; the LORD is his name.)

6

Are ye not as the children of the Ethiopians unto me, O children of Israel? saith the LORD. Have not I brought up Israel out of the land of Egypt, and the Philistines from Caphtor, and the Syrians from Kir? Behold, the eyes of the Lord GOD are upon the sinful kingdom, and I will destroy it from off the face of the earth.

Saving that I will not utterly destroy the house of Jacob, saith the LORD. For, lo, I will command, and I will sift the house of Israel among all the nations, like as corn is sifted in a sieve, yet shall not the least grain fall upon the earth. All the sinners of my people shall die by the sword, which say, The evil shall not overtake nor prevent us.

7

In that day will I raise up the tabernacle of David that is fallen, and close up the breaches thereof; and I will raise up his ruins, and I will build it as in the days of old; that they may possess the remnant of Edom, and all the nations, which are called by my name, saith the LORD that doeth this. Behold, the days come, saith the LORD, that the plowman shall overtake the reaper, and the treader of grapes him that soweth seed; and the mountains shall drop sweet wine, and all the hills shall melt. And I will bring again the captivity of my people Israel, and they shall build the waste cities, and inhabit them; and they shall plant vineyards, and drink the wine thereof; they shall also make gardens, and eat the fruit of them. And I will plant them upon their land, and they shall no more be plucked up out of their land which I have given them, saith the LORD thy God.

The Vision

of

OBADIAH

OBADIAH

DOOM OF EDOM

DOOM OF EDOM

We have heard tidings from the LORD,
And an ambassador is sent among the nations:
    Arise ye, and let us rise up against her in battle.
" Behold, I have made thee small among the nations,
    " Thou art greatly despised.
" The pride of thine heart hath deceived thee,
    " O thou that dwellest in the clefts of the rock :
" Whose habitation is high,
    " That saith in his heart, Who shall bring me down
      to the ground?
" Though thou mount on high as the eagle,
" And though thy nest be set among the stars,
    " I will bring thee down from thence," saith the
      LORD.

If thieves came to thee,
    If robbers by night,
(How art thou cut off!)
    Would they not steal till they had enough?
If grapegatherers came to thee,
    Would they not leave some gleaning grapes?

How are the things of Esau searched out!
 How are his hidden treasures sought up!
All the men of thy confederacy have driven thee out,
 Even to the border;
The men that were at peace with thee have deceived
 thee,
 And prevailed against thee;
They that eat thy bread lay a snare under thee,
 There is none understanding of it.

Shall I not in that day, saith the LORD, destroy the wise men out of Edom, and understanding out of the mount of Esau? And thy mighty men, O Teman, shall be dismayed, to the end that every one may be cut off from the mount of Esau by slaughter. For the violence done to thy brother Jacob shame shall cover thee, and thou shalt be cut off for ever. In the day that thou stoodest on the other side, in the day that strangers carried away his substance, and foreigners entered into his gates, and cast lots upon Jerusalem, even thou wast as one of them. But look not thou on the day of thy brother in the day of his disaster, and rejoice not over the children of Judah in the day of their destruction; neither speak proudly in the day of distress. Enter not into the gate of my people in the day of their calamity; yea, look not thou on their affliction in the day of their calamity, neither lay ye hands on their substance in the day of their calamity. And stand thou not in the crossway, to cut off those of his that escape: and deliver not up those of his that remain in the day of distress. For the day of the LORD is near upon all the nations: as thou hast done, it shall be done unto thee; thy dealing shall return upon thine own head. For as ye have drunk upon my holy mountain, so shall all the nations drink continually, yea, they shall drink, and swallow down, and shall be as though they had not been.

But in mount Zion there shall be those that escape, and it shall be holy; and the house of Jacob shall possess their possessions. And the house of Jacob shall be a fire, and the house of Joseph a flame: and the house of Esau for stubble, and they shall burn among them, and devour them: and there shall not be any remaining to the house of Esau; for the LORD hath spoken it. And they of the South shall possess the mount of Esau; and they of the lowland the Philistines: and they shall possess the field of Ephraim, and the field of Samaria: and Benjamin shall possess Gilead. And the captivity of this host of the children of Israel, which are among the Canaanites, shall possess even unto Zarephath; and the captivity of Jerusalem, which is in Sepharad, shall possess the cities of the South. And saviours shall come up on mount Zion to judge the mount of Esau; and the kingdom shall be the LORD'S.

THE BOOK

OF

JONAH

THE PROPHETIC STORY OF JONAH

i

The Flight to Tarshish

Now the word of the LORD came unto Jonah the son of
Amittai, saying, Arise, go to Nineveh, that great city, and
cry against it; for their wickedness is come up before me.
But Jonah rose up to flee unto Tarshish from the presence
of the LORD. And he went down to Joppa, and found a
ship going to Tarshish; so he paid the fare thereof, and
went down into it, to go with them unto Tarshish from the
presence of the LORD. But the LORD hurled a great wind
into the sea, and there was a mighty tempest in the sea, so
that the ship was like to be broken. Then the mariners
were afraid, and cried every man unto his god; and they
cast forth the wares that were in the ship into the sea, to
lighten it unto them. But Jonah was gone down into the
innermost parts of the ship; and he lay, and was fast
asleep. So the shipmaster came to him, and said unto
him, What meanest thou, O sleeper? arise, call upon thy
God, if so be that God will think upon us, that we perish
not. And they said every one to his fellow, Come, and
let us cast lots, that we may know for whose cause this
evil is upon us. So they cast lots, and the lot fell upon

Jonah. Then said they unto him, Tell us, we pray thee, for whose cause this evil is upon us; what is thine occupation? and whence comest thou? what is thy country? and of what people art thou? And he said unto them, I am an Hebrew; and I fear the LORD, the God of heaven, which hath made the sea and the dry land. Then were the men exceedingly afraid, and said unto him, What is this that thou hast done? (For the men knew that he fled from the presence of the LORD, because he had told them.) Then said they unto him, What shall we do unto thee, that the sea may be calm unto us? for the sea grew more and more tempestuous. And he said unto them, Take me up, and cast me forth into the sea; so shall the sea be calm unto you: for I know that for my sake this great tempest is upon you. Nevertheless the men rowed hard to get them back to the land, but they could not: for the sea grew more and more tempestuous against them. Wherefore they cried unto the LORD, and said, We beseech thee, O LORD, we beseech thee, let us not perish for this man's life, and lay not upon us innocent blood: for thou, O LORD, hast done as it pleased thee. So they took up Jonah, and cast him forth into the sea: and the sea ceased from her raging. Then the men feared the LORD exceedingly; and they offered a sacrifice unto the LORD, and made vows.

ii

The Prayer of Jonah

I called out of mine affliction unto the LORD,
    And he answered me;
Out of the belly * of hell cried I,
    And thou heardest my voice.

For thou didst cast me into the depth,
    In the heart of the seas;
And the flood was round about me,
    All thy waves and thy billows passed over me.

And I said, I am cast out from before thine eyes :
    Yet I will look again toward thy holy temple.
The waters compassed me about,
    Even to the soul.

The deep was round about me;
    The weeds were wrapped about my head.
I went down to the bottoms of the mountains;
    The earth with her bars closed upon me for ever.

* And the LORD prepared a great fish to swallow up Jonah; and Jonah was in the belly of the fish three days and three nights. Then Jonah prayed unto the LORD his God out of the fish's belly.

Yet hast thou brought up my life from the pit, O LORD
    my God:
    When my soul fainted within me, I remembered the
        LORD:
And my prayer came in unto thee,
    Into thine holy temple.

They that regard lying vanities forsake their own
    mercy:
But I will sacrifice unto thee with the voice of thanks-
    giving;
I will pay that which I have vowed:
    Salvation is of the LORD.*

iii

The Preaching at Nineveh

And the word of the LORD came unto Jonah the second
time, saying, Arise, go unto Nineveh, that great city, and
preach unto it the preaching that I bid thee. So Jonah
arose, and went unto Nineveh, according to the word of
the LORD. Now Nineveh was an exceeding great city,
of three days' journey. And Jonah began to enter into

* And the LORD spake unto the fish, and it vomited out Jonah upon the
dry land.

the city a day's journey, and he cried, and said, Yet forty days, and Nineveh shall be overthrown. And the people of Nineveh believed God; and they proclaimed a fast, and put on sackcloth, from the greatest of them even to the least of them. And the tidings reached the king of Nineveh, and he arose from his throne, and laid his robe from him, and covered him with sackcloth, and sat in ashes. And he made proclamation and published through Nineveh, by the decree of the king and his nobles, saying: 'Let neither man nor beast, herd nor flock, taste any thing: let them not feed, nor drink water: but let them be covered with sackcloth, both man and beast, and let them cry mightily unto God: yea, let them turn every one from his evil way, and from the violence that is in their hands. Who knoweth whether God will not turn and repent, and turn away from his fierce anger, that we perish not?' And God saw their works, that they turned from their evil way; and God repented of the evil, which he said he would do unto them: and he did it not.

But it displeased Jonah exceedingly, and he was angry. And he prayed unto the LORD, and said, I pray thee, O LORD, was not this my saying, when I was yet in my country? Therefore I hasted to flee unto Tarshish: for I knew that thou art a gracious God, and full of compassion, slow to anger, and plenteous in mercy, and repentest thee of the evil. Therefore now, O LORD, take, I beseech thee, my life from me; for it is better for me to die than to live.

And the LORD said, Doest thou well to be angry? Then Jonah went out of the city, and sat on the east side of the city, and there made him a booth, and sat under it in the shadow, till he might see what would become of the city. And the LORD God prepared a gourd, and made it to come up over Jonah, that it might be a shadow over his head, to deliver him from his evil case. So Jonah was exceeding glad because of the gourd. But God prepared a worm when the morning rose the next day, and it smote the gourd, that it withered. And it came to pass, when the sun arose, that God prepared a sultry east wind; and the sun beat upon the head of Jonah, that he fainted, and requested for himself that he might die, and said, It is better for me to die than to live. And God said to Jonah, Doest thou well to be angry for the gourd? And he said, I do well to be angry even unto death. And the LORD said: Thou hast had pity on the gourd, for the which thou hast not laboured, neither madest it grow; which came up in a night, and perished in a night: and should not I have pity on Nineveh, that great city; wherein are more than sixscore thousand persons that cannot discern between their right hand and their left hand; and also much cattle?

The Word of the LORD

that came to

MICAH

the Morashtite

in the days of

Jotham

Ahaz

and Hezekiah

kings of Judah

which he saw concerning

Samaria and Jerusalem

MICAH

i

A Discourse of Judgment and Salvation

Hear, ye peoples, all of you; hearken, O earth, and all
that therein is: and let the Lord GOD be witness among
you, the Lord from his holy temple. For, behold, the
LORD cometh forth out of his place, and will come down,
and tread upon the high places of the earth. And the
mountains shall be molten under him, and the valleys
shall be cleft, as wax before the fire, as waters that are
poured down a steep place. For the transgression of
Jacob is all this, and for the sins of the house of Israel.
What is the transgression of Jacob? is it not Samaria?
and what are the high places of Judah? are they not Jerusalem? Therefore I will make Samaria as an heap of the
field, and as the plantings of a vineyard: and I will pour
down the stones thereof into the valley, and I will discover
the foundations thereof. And all her graven images shall
be beaten to pieces, and all her hires shall be burned with
fire, and all her idols will I lay desolate: for of the hire of
an harlot hath she gathered them, and unto the hire of an
harlot shall they return.

2

For this will I wail and howl;
  I will go stripped and naked:
  I will make a wailing like the jackals,
  And a mourning like the ostriches.

For her wounds are incurable:
  For it is come even unto Judah;
  It reacheth to the gate of my people,
  Even to Jerusalem.

Tell it not in Gath:
  Weep not at all;
  At Beth-le-Aphrah roll thyself in the dust;
  Pass ye away, O inhabitant of Shaphir, in nakedness
    and shame.

The inhabitant of Zaanan is not come forth;
  The wailing of Beth-ezel shall take from you the
    stay thereof;
  For the inhabitant of Maroth waiteth anxiously for
    good:
  Because evil is come down from the LORD unto the
    gate of Jerusalem.

Bind the chariot to the 'swift steed,' O inhabitant of
    'Lachish':
  She was the beginning of sin to the daughter of Zion,
  For the transgressions of Israel were found in thee.

Therefore shalt thou give a parting gift to Moresheth-
    gath;
The houses of 'Achzib' shall be 'a deceitful thing'
    unto the kings of Israel;
I will yet bring unto thee, O inhabitant of 'Mare-
    shah,' him that shall 'possess' thee.

The glory of Israel shall come even unto Adullam:
    Make thee bald and poll thee for the children of
        thy delight;
    Enlarge thy baldness as the eagle:
    For they are gone into captivity from thee.

3

Woe to them that devise iniquity and work evil upon
their beds! when the morning is light, they practise it,
because it is in the power of their hand. And they covet
fields, and seize them; and houses, and take them away:
and they oppress a man and his house, even a man and
his heritage. Therefore thus saith the LORD: Behold,
against this family do I devise an evil, from which ye shall
not remove your necks, neither shall ye walk haughtily;
for it is an evil time. In that day shall they take up a
parable against you, and lament with a doleful lamentation,
and say:

We be utterly spoiled:
    He changeth the portion of my people:

How doth he remove it from me!
To the rebellious he divideth our fields.

Therefore thou shalt have none that shall cast the line by lot in the congregation of the LORD.

4

Prophesy ye not — thus they prophesy — *they shall not prophesy of these things: their reproaches never cease!* — Shall it be said, O house of Jacob, Is the spirit of the LORD straitened? are these his doings? Do not my words do good to him that walketh uprightly? But of late my people is risen up as an enemy: ye strip the robe from off the garment from them that pass by securely as men averse from war. The women of my people ye cast out from their pleasant houses; from their young children ye take away my glory for ever. Arise ye, and depart; for this is not your rest: because of uncleanness that destroyeth, even with a grievous destruction.

If a man walking in wind and falsehood do lie, saying, I will prophesy unto thee of wine and of strong drink; he shall even be the prophet of this people.

'I will surely assemble, O Jacob, all of thee;
I will surely gather the remnant of Israel:
I will put them together as the sheep of Bozrah:
As a flock in the midst of their pasture.

They shall make great noise by reason of the multitude
of men :
The breaker is gone up before them ;
They have broken forth and passed on to the gate,
And are gone out thereat ;
And their king is passed on before them,
And the LORD at the head of them.'

And I said, Hear, I pray you, ye heads of Jacob and
rulers of the house of Israel : is it not for you to know
judgement? who hate the good, and love the evil; who
pluck off their skin from off them, and their flesh from off
their bones ; who also eat the flesh of my people ; and they
flay their skin from off them, and break their bones : yea,
they chop them in pieces, as for the pot, and as flesh
within the caldron.   Then shall they cry unto the LORD,
but he will not answer them : yea, he will hide his face
from them at that time, according as they have wrought
evil in their doings.   Thus saith the LORD concerning the
prophets that make my people to err ; that bite with their
teeth and cry, Peace ; and whoso putteth not into their
mouths, they even prepare war against him : Therefore it
shall be night unto you, that ye shall have no vision ; and
it shall be dark unto you, that ye shall not divine ; and the
sun shall go down upon the prophets, and the day shall be
black over them.   And the seers shall be ashamed, and
the diviners confounded ; yea, they shall all cover their

lips: for there is no answer of God. But I truly am full of power by the spirit of the LORD, and of judgement, and of might, to declare unto Jacob his transgression, and to Israel his sin.

5

Hear this, I pray you, ye heads of the house of Jacob, and rulers of the house of Israel, that abhor judgement, and pervert all equity. They build up Zion with blood, and Jerusalem with iniquity. The heads thereof judge for reward, and the priests thereof teach for hire, and the prophets thereof divine for money: yet will they lean upon the LORD, and say, Is not the LORD in the midst of us? no evil shall come upon us. Therefore shall Zion for your sake be plowed as a field, and Jerusalem shall become heaps, and the mountain of the house as the high places of a forest.

6

But in the latter days it shall come to pass, that the mountain of the LORD'S house shall be established at the head of the mountains, and it shall be exalted above the hills; and peoples shall flow unto it. And many nations shall go and say, Come ye, and let us go up to the mountain of the LORD, and to the house of the God of Jacob; and he will teach us of his ways, and we will walk in his paths: for out of Zion shall go forth the law, and the word of the LORD from Jerusalem. And he shall judge between many peoples, and shall reprove strong nations afar off; and they shall beat their swords into plowshares, and their spears into pruninghooks: nation shall not lift up sword against nation, neither shall they learn war any more. But they shall sit every man under his vine and under his fig tree; and none shall make them afraid: for the mouth of the LORD of hosts hath spoken it. For all the peoples will walk every one in the name of his god, and we will walk in the name of the LORD our God for ever and ever. In that day, saith the LORD, will I assemble her that halteth, and I will gather her that is driven away, and her that I have afflicted; and I will make her that halted a remnant, and her that was cast far off a strong nation: and the LORD shall reign over them in mount Zion from henceforth even for ever. And thou, O tower of the flock, the hill of the daughter of Zion, unto thee shall it come; yea, the former dominion shall come, the kingdom of the daughter of Jerusalem.

7

Now why dost thou cry out aloud? Is there no king in thee, is thy counsellor perished, that pangs have taken hold of thee as of a woman in travail? Be in pain, and labour to bring forth, O daughter of Zion, like a woman in travail: for now shalt thou go forth out of the city, and shalt dwell in the field, and shalt come even unto Babylon; there shalt thou be rescued; there shall the LORD redeem thee from the hand of thine enemies.

And now many nations are assembled against thee, that say, Let her be defiled, and let our eye see its desire upon Zion. But they know not the thoughts of the LORD, neither understand they his counsel: for he hath gathered them as the sheaves to the threshing-floor. Arise and thresh, O daughter of Zion: for I will make thine horn iron, and I will make thy hoofs brass: and thou shalt beat in pieces many peoples: and thou shalt devote their gain unto the LORD, and their substance unto the Lord of the whole earth.

Now shalt thou gather thyself in troops, O daughter of troops: 'he hath laid siege against us: they shall smite the judge of Israel with a rod upon the cheek.' But thou, Beth-lehem Ephrathah, which art little to be among the thousands of Judah, out of thee shall one come forth unto me that is to be ruler in Israel: whose goings forth are from of old, from ancient days. Therefore will he give them up, until the time that she which travaileth hath brought forth: then the residue of his brethren shall return with the children of Israel. And he shall stand, and shall feed his flock in the strength of the LORD, in the majesty of the name of the LORD his God: and they shall abide; for now shall he be great unto the ends of the earth. And this man shall be our peace: when the Assyrian shall come into our land, and when he shall tread in our palaces, then shall we raise against him seven shepherds, and eight principal men. And they shall waste

138

the land of Assyria with the sword and the land of Nimrod
in the entrances thereof: and he shall deliver us from the
Assyrian, when he cometh into our land, and when he
treadeth within our border. And the remnant of Jacob
shall be in the midst of many peoples as dew from the
LORD, as showers upon the grass; that tarrieth not for
man, nor waiteth for the sons of men. And the remnant
of Jacob shall be among the nations, in the midst of many
peoples, as a lion among the beasts of the forest, as a
young lion among the flocks of sheep : who, if he go through,
treadeth down and teareth in pieces, and there is none to
deliver.

Let thine hand be lifted up above thine adversaries ;
And let all thine enemies be cut off!

And it shall come to pass in that day, saith the LORD,
that I will cut off thy horses out of the midst of thee, and
will destroy thy chariots : and I will cut off the cities of
thy land, and will throw down all thy strong holds : and
I will cut off witchcrafts out of thine hand ; and thou shalt
have no more soothsayers : and I will cut off thy graven
images and thy pillars out of the midst of thee ; and thou
shalt no more worship the work of thine hands. And I
will pluck up thine Asherim out of the midst of thee : and
I will destroy thy cities. And I will execute vengeance in
anger and fury upon the nations which hearken not.

ii

The LORD'S Controversy before the Mountains

Hear ye now what the LORD saith:

THE LORD

Arise, contend thou before the mountains, and let the hills hear thy voice. Hear, O ye mountains, the LORD'S controversy, and ye enduring foundations of the earth: for the LORD hath a controversy with his people, and he will plead with Israel.

O my people, what have I done unto thee? and wherein have I wearied thee? testify against me. For I brought thee up out of the land of Egypt, and redeemed thee out of the house of bondage; and I sent before thee Moses, Aaron, and Miriam. O my people, remember now what Balak king of Moab consulted, and what Balaam the son of Beor answered him; remember from Shittim unto Gilgal, that ye may know the righteous acts of the LORD.

THE PEOPLE

Wherewith shall I come before the LORD, and bow myself before the high God? shall I come before him with burnt offerings, with calves of a year old? Will the LORD be pleased with thousands of rams or with ten thousands

of rivers of oil?   Shall I give my firstborn for my transgression, the fruit of my body for the sin of my soul?

THE MOUNTAINS

He hath shewed thee, O man, what is good ; and what
doth the LORD require of thee, but to do justly, and to love
mercy, and to walk humbly with thy God?

iii

The LORD'S Cry and the Man of Wisdom

*The voice of the LORD crieth unto the city, and the
Man of Wisdom will see thy name.*

THE LORD

Hear ye the rod, and who hath appointed it.   Are there
yet the treasures of wickedness in the house of the wicked,
and the scant measure that is abominable?   Shall I be pure
with wicked balances, and with a bag of deceitful weights?
For the rich men thereof aie full of violence, and the
inhabitants thereof have spoken lies, and their tongue is
deceitful in their mouth.   Therefore I also have smitten
thee with a grievous wound ; I have made thee desolate
because of thy sins.   Thou shalt eat, but not be satisfied ;
and thy humiliation shall be in the midst of thee : and

thou shalt remove, but shalt not carry away safe; and that
which thou carriest away will I give up to the sword.
Thou shalt sow, but shalt not reap: thou shalt tread the
olives, but shalt not anoint thee with oil; and the vintage, but shalt not drink the wine. For the statutes of
Omri are kept, and all the works of the house of Ahab,
and ye walk in their counsels: that I should make thee a
desolation, and the inhabitants thereof an hissing; and ye
shall bear the reproach of my people.

THE DESPAIRING PEOPLE

Woe is me! for I am as when they have gathered the
summer fruits, as the grape gleanings of the vintage: there
is no cluster to eat; nor firstripe fig which my soul desired.
The godly man is perished out of the earth, and there is
none upright among men: they all lie in wait for blood;
they hunt every man his brother with a net. Both hands
are put forth for evil to do it diligently; the prince asketh,
and the judge is ready for a reward; and the great man,
he uttereth the mischief of his soul: thus they weave it
together. The best of them is as a brier: the most upright
is worse than a thorn hedge: the day of thy watchmen,
even thy visitation, is come; now shall be their perplexity.
Trust ye not in a friend, put ye not confidence in a guide:
keep the doors of thy mouth from her that lieth in thy
bosom. For the son dishonoureth the father, the daughter

riseth up against her mother, the daughter in law against her mother in law; a man's enemies are the men of his own house.

THE MAN OF WISDOM

But as for me, I will look unto the LORD; I will wait for the God of my salvation: my God will hear me. Rejoice not against me, O mine enemy: when I fall, I shall arise; when I sit in darkness, the LORD shall be a light unto me. I will bear the indignation of the LORD, because I have sinned against him; until he plead my cause, and execute judgement for me: he will bring me forth to the light, and I shall behold his righteousness. Then mine enemy shall see it, and shame shall cover her; which said unto me, Where is the LORD thy God? Mine eyes shall behold her; now shall she be trodden down as the mire of the streets.

THE LORD

A day for building thy walls! in that day shall the decree be far removed. In that day shall they come unto thee, from Assyria and the cities of Egypt, and from Egypt even to the River, and from sea to sea, and from mountain to mountain.

Yet shall the land be desolate because of them that dwell therein, for the fruit of their doings.

The Man of Wisdom

Feed thy people with thy rod, the flock of thine heritage, which dwell solitarily, in the forest in the midst of Carmel: let them feed in Bashan and Gilead, as in the days of old.

The Lord

As in the days of thy coming forth out of the land of Egypt will I shew unto him marvellous things.

The Man of Wisdom

The nations shall see and be ashamed of all their might: they shall lay their hand upon their mouth, their ears shall be deaf. They shall lick the dust like a serpent; like crawling things of the earth they shall come trembling out of their close places: they shall come with fear unto the Lord our God, and shall be afraid because of thee.

Who is a God like unto thee, that pardoneth iniquity, and passeth by the transgression of the remnant of his heritage? he retaineth not his anger for ever, because he delighteth in mercy. He will turn again and have compassion upon us; he will tread our iniquities under foot: and thou wilt cast all their sins into the depths of the sea. Thou wilt perform the truth to Jacob, and the mercy to Abraham, which thou hast sworn unto our fathers from the days of old.

144

The Oracle concerning

NINEVEH

The Book of the Vision of

NAHUM

the Elkoshite

NAHUM

DOOM OF NINEVEH

DOOM OF NINEVEH

The LORD is a jealous God and avengeth; the LORD
avengeth and is full of wrath; the LORD taketh vengeance
on his adversaries, and he reserveth wrath for his enemies.
The LORD is slow to anger, and great in power, and will
by no means clear the guilty: the LORD hath his way in
the whirlwind and in the storm, and the clouds are the
dust of his feet. He rebuketh the sea, and maketh it dry,
and drieth up all the rivers: Bashan languisheth, and
Carmel, and the flower of Lebanon languisheth. The
mountains quake at him, and the hills melt; and the earth
is upheaved at his presence, yea, the world, and all that
dwell therein. Who can stand before his indignation?
and who can abide in the fierceness of his anger? his fury
is poured out like fire, and the rocks are broken asunder
by him.

The LORD is good, a strong hold in the day of trouble;
and he knoweth them that put their trust in him.

But with an overrunning flood he will make a full end
of the place thereof, and will pursue his enemies into darkness.

What do ye imagine against the LORD? he will make a full end: affliction shall not rise up the second time. For though they be like tangled thorns, and be drenched as it were in their drink, they shall be devoured utterly as dry stubble. There is one gone forth out of thee, that imagineth evil against the LORD, that counselleth wickedness. Thus saith the LORD: Though they be in full strength, and likewise many, even so shall they be cut down, and he shall pass away.

Though I have afflicted thee, I will afflict thee no more. And now will I break his yoke from off thee, and will burst thy bonds in sunder.

And the LORD hath given commandment concerning thee, that no more of thy name be sown; out of the house of thy gods will I cut off the graven image and the molten image; I will make thy grave; for thou art vile.

3

Behold, upon the mountains the feet of him that bringeth good tidings, that publisheth peace! Keep thy feasts, O Judah, perform thy vows: for the wicked one shall no more pass through thee; he is utterly cut off.

He that dasheth in pieces is come up before thy face:
Keep the munition; watch the way;

Nahum ℞

Make thy loins strong,
    Fortify thy power mightily.

For the LORD bringeth again the excellency of Jacob, as the excellency of Israel: for the emptiers have emptied them out, and marred their vine branches.

The shield of his mighty men is made red:
    The valiant men are in scarlet:
The chariots flash with steel in the day of his prepara-
    tion,
    And the spears are shaken terribly.

The chariots rage in the streets,
    They justle one against another in the broad ways:
The appearance of them is like torches,
    They run like the lightnings.

He remembereth his worthies:
    They stumble in their march;
They make haste to the wall thereof,
    And the mantelet is prepared.

The gates of the rivers are opened, and the palace is
    dissolved:
    And Huzzab is uncovered; she is carried away;
And her handmaids mourn as with the voice of doves,
    Tabering upon their breasts.

But Nineveh hath been from of old like a pool of
    water;
    Yet they flee away:
'Stand, stand'—
    But none looketh back.

Take ye the spoil of silver,
    Take the spoil of gold;
For there is none end of the store,
    The glory of all pleasant furniture.

She is empty, and void, and waste:
    And the heart melteth, and the knees smite to-
    gether;
And anguish is in all loins,
    And the faces of them all are waxed pale.

4

Where is the den of the lions,
    And the feeding place of the young lions,
Where the lion and the lioness walked,
    The lion's whelp, and none made them afraid?

The lion did tear in pieces enough for his whelps,
    And strangled for his lionesses;
And filled his caves with prey,   '
    And his dens with ravin.

5

Behold, I am against thee, saith the LORD of hosts, and
I will burn her chariots in the smoke, and the sword shall
devour thy young lions: and I will cut off thy prey from
the earth, and the voice of thy messengers shall no more
be heard.

Woe to the bloody city!
It is all full of lies and rapine;
The prey departeth not.

The noise of the whip, and the noise of the rattling of
    wheels;
And pransing horses, and jumping chariots;
The horseman mounting, and the flashing sword, and
    the glittering spear;

And a multitude of slain, and a great heap of carcases:
And there is none end of the corpses;
They stumble upon their corpses:

Because of the multitude of the whoredoms of the well-
    favoured harlot,
The mistress of witchcrafts, that selleth nations through
    her whoredoms,
And families through her witchcrafts.

Behold, I am against thee, saith the LORD of hosts, and
I will discover thy skirts upon thy face; and I will shew
the nations thy nakedness, and the kingdoms thy shame.
And I will cast abominable filth upon thee, and make thee
vile, and will set thee as a gazingstock.   And it shall
come to pass, that all they that look upon thee shall flee
from thee, and say ·

<h2 style="text-align:center">6</h2>

Nineveh is laid waste: who will bemoan her?
Whence shall I seek comforters for thee?

Art thou better than No-amon, that was situate among
    the rivers,
    That had the waters round about her;
Whose rampart was the sea,
    And her wall was of the sea?

Ethiopia and Egypt were her strength, and it was
    infinite;
    Put and Lubim were thy helpers:
Yet was she carried away, she went into captivity:
    Her young children also were dashed in pieces at
    the top of all the streets;

And they cast lots for her honourable men,
    And all her great men were bound in chains:

Thou also shalt be drunken, thou shalt be hid;
    Thou also shalt seek a strong hold because of the
      enemy.

All thy fortresses shall be like fig trees with the first-
      ripe figs:
If they be shaken,
They fall into the mouth of the eater.

Behold, thy people in the midst of thee are women;
The gates of thy land are set wide open unto thine
      enemies;
The fire hath devoured thy bars.

Draw the water for the siege;
    Strengthen thy fortresses:
Go into the clay, and tread the mortar, make strong the
      brickkiln:
    There shall the fire devour thee; the sword shall
      cut thee off.

It shall devour thee like the cankerworm:
    Make thyself many as the cankerworm, make thy-
      self many as the locust;
Thou hast multiplied thy merchants above the stars of
      heaven:
    The cankerworm spreadeth himself, and flieth away.

Thy crowned are as the locusts, and thy marshals as
  the swarms of grasshoppers,
 Which camp in the hedges in the cold day,
But when the sun ariseth they flee away,
  And their place is not known where they are.

7

Thy shepherds slumber, O king of Assyria,
  Thy worthies are at rest:
Thy people are scattered upon the mountains,
  And there is none to gather them.

There is no assuaging of thy hurt;
  Thy wound is grievous:
All that hear the bruit of thee clap the hands over
  thee:
  For upon whom hath not thy wickedness passed
  continually?

The Oracle which

HABAKKUK

the Prophet did see

HABAKKUK

A RHAPSODY OF THE CHALDEANS

A RHAPSODY OF THE CHALDEANS

i

The Mystery

THE PROPHET

O LORD, how long shall I cry, and thou wilt not hear? I cry out unto thee of violence, and thou wilt not save. Why dost thou shew me iniquity, and cause me to look upon perverseness? for spoiling and violence are before me: and there is strife, and contention riseth up. Therefore the law is slacked, and judgement doth never go forth: for the wicked doth compass about the righteous; therefore judgement goeth forth perverted.

THE LORD

Behold ye among the nations, and regard, and wonder marvellously: for I work a work in your days, which ye will not believe though it be told you. For, lo, I raise up the Chaldeans, that bitter and hasty nation; which march through the breadth of the earth, to possess dwelling places that are not theirs. They are terrible and dreadful:

their judgement and their dignity proceed from themselves. Their horses also are swifter than leopards, and are more fierce than the evening wolves; and their horsemen bear themselves proudly: yea, their horsemen come from far; they fly as an eagle that hasteth to devour. They come all of them for violence; their faces are set eagerly as the east wind; and they gather captives as the sand. Yea, he scoffeth at kings, and princes are a derision unto him: he derideth every strong hold; for he heapeth up dust, and taketh it. Then shall he sweep by as a wind, and shall pass over, and be guilty: even he whose might is his god.

The Prophet

Art not thou from everlasting, O Lord my God, mine Holy One? thou diest not. O Lord, thou hast ordained him for judgement; and thou, O Rock, hast established him for correction. Thou that art of purer eyes than to behold evil, and that canst not look on perverseness, wherefore lookest thou upon them that deal treacherously, and holdest thy peace when the wicked swalloweth up the man that is more righteous than he; and makest men as the fishes of the sea, as the creeping things, that have no ruler over them? He taketh up all of them with the angle, he catcheth them in his net, and gathereth them in his drag: therefore he rejoiceth and is glad. Therefore he sacrificeth unto his net, and burneth incense unto his drag; because by them his portion is fat, and his meat plenteous. Shall he therefore empty his net, and not spare to slay the nations continually?

ii

The Solution

THE PROPHET

I will stand upon my watch, and set me upon the tower, and will look forth to see what he will speak by me, and what I shall answer concerning my complaint.

THE LORD

Write the vision, and make it plain upon tables, that he may run that readeth it. For the vision is yet for the appointed time, and it hasteth toward the end, and shall not lie: though it tarry, wait for it; because it will surely come, it will not delay. Behold, his soul is puffed up, it is not upright in him: but the just shall live in his faithfulness. Yea, moreover, wine is a treacherous dealer, a haughty man, and that keepeth not at home; who enlargeth his desire as hell, and he is as death, and cannot be satisfied, but gathereth unto him all nations, and heap-

eth unto him all peoples. Shall not all these take up a
parable against him, and a taunting proverb against him,
and say:

Doom of the Chaldeans

1

WOE to him that increaseth that which is not his,
— How long? —
And that ladeth himself with pledges!

Shall they not rise up suddenly that shall exact usury
of thee, and awake that shall vex thee, and thou shalt be
for booties unto them? Because thou hast spoiled many
nations, all the remnant of the peoples shall spoil thee;
because of men's blood, and for the violence done to the
land, to the city, and to all that dwell therein.

2

WOE to him that getteth an evil gain for his house,
That he may set his nest on high,
That he may be delivered from the hand of evil!

Thou hast consulted shame to thy house by cutting off
many peoples, and hast sinned against thy soul. For the
stone shall cry out of the wall, and the beam out of the
timber shall answer it.

3

WOE to him that buildeth a town with blood,
And stablisheth a city by iniquity!

Behold, is it not of the LORD of hosts that the peoples
labour for the fire, and the nations weary themselves for
vanity? For the earth shall be filled with the knowledge
of the glory of the LORD, as the waters cover the sea.

4

WOE unto him that giveth his neighbour drink,
That addest thy venom thereto,
And makest him drunken also,
That thou mayest look on their nakedness!

Thou art filled with shame for glory: drink thou also,
and be as one uncircumcised. The cup of the LORD's
right hand shall be turned unto thee, and foul shame shall
be upon thy glory. For the violence done to Lebanon
shall cover thee, and the destruction of the beasts which
made them afraid; because of men's blood, and for the
violence done to the land, to the city, and to all that dwell
therein.

5

What profiteth the graven image, that the maker thereof
hath graven it; the molten image, and the teacher of lies,
that the maker of his work trusteth therein, to make dumb
idols? —

WOE unto him that saith to the wood, Awake;
To the dumb stone, Arise!

Shall this teach? Behold, it is laid over with gold and
silver, and there is no breath at all in the midst of it. But
the LORD is in his holy temple: let all the earth keep
silence before him!

iii

Jehovah come to Judgment *

. *Prelude*

O LORD, I have heard the report of thee, and am
   afraid:
O LORD, revive thy work in the midst of the years,
In the midst of the years make it known:
In wrath remember mercy!

Strophe

God cometh from Teman,
And the Holy One from Mount Paran.
His glory covereth the heavens,
And the earth is full of his praise.
And his brightness is as the light;

* A prayer of Habakkuk the prophet, set to Shigionoth.

He hath rays coming forth from his hand;
And there is the hiding of his power.
Before him goeth the pestilence,
And fiery bolts go forth at his feet.
He standeth and shaketh the earth;
He beholdeth, and driveth asunder the nations:
And the eternal mountains are scattered,
The everlasting hills do bow;
His ways are everlasting.
I see the tents of Cushan in affliction;
The curtains of the land of Midian do tremble.

Antistrophe

Is the LORD displeased against the rivers?
Is thine anger against the rivers, or thy wrath against
    the sea,
That thou dost ride upon thine horses,
Upon thy chariots of salvation?
Thy bow is made quite bare,
Sworn are the chastisements of thy word.
Thou dost cleave the earth with rivers;
The mountains see thee and are afraid;
The tempest of waters passeth by;
The deep uttereth his voice,
And lifteth up his hands on high;
The sun and moon stand still in their habitation

At the light of thine arrows as they go,
At the shining of thy glittering spear.
Thou dost march through the land in indignation,
Thou dost thresh the nations in anger.

Epode

Thou art come for the salvation of thy people,
For the salvation of thine anointed:
Thou dost smite off the head from the house of the
    wicked,
Laying bare the foundation even unto the neck.
Thou dost pierce with his own staves the head of his
    warriors:
(They came as a whirlwind to scatter me,
Their rejoicing was as to devour the poor secretly:)
Thou didst tread the sea with thine horses, the surge
    of mighty waters.

Postlude

I heard, and my belly trembled,
My lips quivered at the voice;
Rottenness entered into my bones, and I trembled in
    my place:
That I should rest waiting for the day of trouble,
When he that shall invade them in troops cometh up
    against the people.

Habakkuk &c—

For though the fig tree shall not blossom,
Neither shall fruit be in the vines;
The labour of the olive shall fail,
And the fields shall yield no meat;
The flock shall be cut off from the fold,
And there shall be no herd in the stalls:
Yet I will rejoice in the LORD,
I will joy in the God of my salvation.
Jehovah, the Lord, is my strength,
And he maketh my feet like hinds' feet,
And will make me to walk upon mine high places.*

* For the Chief Musician, on my stringed instruments.

The Word of the LORD

which came unto

ZEPHANIAH

the son of Cushi

the son of Gedaliah, the son of Amariah
the son of Hezekiah

in the days of

Josiah the son of Amon

king of Judah

ZEPHANIAH

THE DAY OF THE LORD

THE DAY OF THE LORD

I will utterly consume all things from off the face of the ground, saith the LORD. I will consume man and beast; I will consume the fowls of the heaven, and the fishes of the sea, and the stumbling-blocks with the wicked; and I will cut off man from off the face of the ground, saith the LORD. And I will stretch out mine hand upon Judah, and upon all the inhabitants of Jerusalem; and I will cut off the remnant of Baal from this place, and the name of the Chemarim with the priests; and them that worship the host of heaven upon the housetops; and them that worship, which swear to the LORD and swear by Malcam; and them that are turned back from following the LORD; and those that have not sought the LORD, nor inquired after him.

Hold thy peace at the presence of the Lord GOD:
   For the Day of the LORD is at hand:
For the LORD hath prepared a sacrifice,
   He hath sanctified his guests!

And it shall come to pass in the day of the LORD's sacrifice, that I will punish the princes, and the king's sons, and all such as are clothed with foreign apparel. And in that day I will punish all those that leap over the threshold, which fill their master's house with violence and deceit. And in that day, saith the LORD, there shall be the noise of a cry from the fish gate, and an howling from the second quarter, and a great crashing from the hills.

Howl, ye inhabitants of The Mortar!
For all the merchant people are undone:
All they that were laden with silver are cut off.

And it shall come to pass at that time, that I will search Jerusalem with candles; and I will punish the men that are settled on their lees, that say in their heart, The LORD will not do good, neither will he do evil. And their wealth shall become a spoil, and their houses a desolation; yea, they shall build houses, but shall not inhabit them; and they shall plant vineyards, but shall not drink the wine thereof.

The great Day of the LORD is near:
It is near and hasteth greatly!
Even the voice of the Day of the LORD;
The mighty man crieth there bitterly!

That Day is a day of wrath,
A day of trouble and distress,
A day of wasteness and desolation,
A day of darkness and gloominess,

Zephaniah ❧

A day of clouds and thick darkness,
   A day of the trumpet and alarm
Against the fenced cities,
   And against the high battlements!

And I will bring distress upon men, that they shall walk
like blind men, because they have sinned against the
LORD: and their blood shall be poured out as dust, and
their flesh as dung. Neither their silver nor their gold
shall be able to deliver them in the day of the LORD's
wrath; but the whole land shall be devoured by the fire
of his jealousy: for he shall make an end, yea, a terrible
end, of all them that dwell in the land.

Gather yourselves together, yea, gather together,
O nation that hath no shame;
   Before the decree bring forth,
   Before the day pass as the chaff,
   Before the fierce anger of the LORD come upon you,
   Before the Day of the LORD's Anger come upon you.

Seek ye the LORD, all ye meek of the earth,
Which have wrought his judgement;
   Seek righteousness,
   Seek meekness:
   It may be ye shall be hid
   In the Day of the LORD's Anger.

2

For Gaza shall be forsaken, and Ashkelon a desolation: they shall drive out Ashdod at the noonday, and Ekron shall be rooted up.

> Woe unto the inhabitants of the sea coast,
> The nation of the Cherethites!

The word of the LORD is against you, O Canaan, the land of the Philistines; I will destroy thee that there shall be no inhabitant. And the sea coast shall be pastures, with cottages for shepherds and folds for flocks. And the coast shall be for the remnant of the house of Judah; they shall feed their flocks thereupon: in the houses of Ashkelon shall they lie down in the evening; for the LORD their God shall visit them, and bring again their captivity. I have heard the reproach of Moab, and the revilings of the children of Ammon, wherewith they have reproached my people, and magnified themselves against their border. Therefore as I live, saith the LORD of hosts, the God of Israel: Surely Moab shall be as Sodom, and the children of Ammon as Gomorrah, a possession of nettles, and saltpits, and a perpetual desolation: the residue of my people shall spoil them, and the remnant of my nation shall inherit them. This shall they have for their pride, because they have reproached and magnified themselves against the people of the LORD of

Zephaniah ❧

hosts. The LORD will be terrible unto them: for he will
famish all the gods of the earth; and men shall worship
him, every one from his place, even all the isles of the
nations. Ye Ethiopians also, ye shall be slain by my
sword. And he will stretch out his hand against the
north, and destroy Assyria; and will make Nineveh
a desolation, and dry like the wilderness. And herds
shall lie down in the midst of her, all the beasts of the
nations: both the pelican and the porcupine shall lodge
in the chapiters thereof: their voice shall sing in the
windows; desolation shall be in the thresholds: for he
hath laid bare the cedar work.

> This is the joyous city,
>> That dwelt carelessly,
>> That said in her heart, I am,
>> And there is none else beside me:
> How is she become a desolation,
> A place for beasts to lie down in!
> Every one that passeth by her shall hiss,
> And wag his hand.

> Woe to her that is rebellious and polluted,
> To the oppressing city!
>> She obeyed not the voice;
>> She received not correction;
>> She trusted not in the LORD;

She drew not near to her God.
Her princes in the midst of her are roaring lions;
Her judges are evening wolves;
They leave nothing till the morrow.
Her prophets are light and treacherous persons:
Her priests have profaned the sanctuary,
They have done violence to the law.
The LORD in the midst of her is righteous;
He will not do iniquity;
Every morning doth he bring his judgement to light,
He faileth not;
But the unjust knoweth no shame.

I have cut off nations, their battlements are desolate;
I have made their streets 'waste, that none passeth by;
their cities are destroyed, so that there is no man, that
there is none inhabitant. I said, Surely thou wilt fear
me, thou wilt receive correction; so her dwelling should
not be cut off, according to all that I have appointed concerning her: but they rose early and corrupted all their
doings. Therefore wait ye for me, saith the LORD, until
the day that I rise up to the prey: for my determination
is to gather the nations, that I may assemble the kingdoms, to pour upon them mine indignation, even all my
fierce anger; for all the earth shall be devoured with the
fire of my jealousy.

3

For then will I turn to the peoples a pure language, that they may all call upon the name of the LORD, to serve him with one consent. From beyond the rivers of Ethiopia my suppliants, even the daughter of my dispersed, shall bring mine offering. In that day shalt thou not be ashamed for all thy doings, wherein thou hast transgressed against me: for then I will take away out of the midst of thee thy proudly exulting ones, and thou shalt no more be haughty in my holy mountain. But I will leave in the midst of thee an afflicted and poor people, and they shall trust in the name of the LORD. The remnant of Israel shall not do iniquity, nor speak lies; neither shall a deceitful tongue be found in their mouth: for they shall feed and lie down, and none shall make them afraid.

Sing, O daughter of Zion; shout, O Israel;
Be glad and rejoice with all the heart, O daughter of
    Jerusalem.
    The LORD hath taken away thy judgements,
    He hath cast out thine enemy:
    The king of Israel, even the LORD, is in the midst
    of thee:
    Thou shalt not fear evil any more.

In that day it shall be said to Jerusalem, Fear thou not:
O Zion, let not thine hands be slack.

→§ Minor Prophets

The LORD thy God is in the midst of thee,
A mighty one who will save:
He will rejoice over thee with joy, he will rest in
    his love,
He will joy over thee with singing.

I will gather them that sorrow for the solemn assembly,
who were of thee: to whom the burden upon her was
a reproach. Behold, at that time I will deal with all them
that afflict thee: and I will save her that halteth, and
gather her that was driven away; and I will make them
a praise and a name, whose shame hath been in all the
earth. At that time will I bring you in, and at that time
will I gather you: for I will make you a name and a
praise among all the peoples of the earth, when I bring
again your captivity before your eyes, saith the LORD.

THE BOOK

OF

HAGGAI

HAGGAI

PROPHECIES TO THE BUILDERS OF THE TEMPLE

PROPHECIES TO THE BUILDERS OF THE TEMPLE

i

In the second year of Darius the king, in the sixth month, in the first day of the month, came the word of the LORD by Haggai the prophet unto Zerubbabel the son of Shealtiel, governor of Judah, and to Joshua the son of Jehozadak, the high priest, saying:

Thus speaketh the LORD of hosts, saying, This people say, It is not the time for us to come, the time for the LORD'S house to be built. Then came the word of the LORD by Haggai the prophet, saying, Is it a time for you yourselves to dwell in your cieled houses, while this house lieth waste? Now therefore thus saith the LORD of hosts: Consider your ways. Ye have sown much, and bring in little; ye eat, but ye have not enough; ye drink, but ye are not filled with drink; ye clothe you, but there is none warm; and he that earneth wages earneth wages to put it into a bag with holes. Thus saith the LORD of hosts: Consider your ways. Go up to the mountain, and bring wood, and build the house; and I will take pleasure in it, and I will be glorified, saith the LORD. Ye looked for much, and lo, it came to little; and when ye brought it home, I did blow upon it. Why? saith the LORD of hosts. Because of

179

mine house that lieth waste, while ye run every man to his own house. Therefore for your sake the heaven is stayed from dew, and the earth is stayed from her fruit. And I called for a drought upon the land, and upon the mountains, and upon the corn, and upon the wine, and upon the oil, and upon that which the ground bringeth forth, and upon men, and upon cattle, and upon all the labour of the hands.

Then Zerubbabel the son of Shealtiel, and Joshua the son of Jehozadak, the high priest, with all the remnant of the people, obeyed the voice of the LORD their God, and the words of Haggai the prophet, as the LORD their God had sent him; and the people did fear before the LORD. Then spake Haggai the LORD's messenger in the LORD's message unto the people, saying, I am with you, saith the LORD. And the LORD stirred up the spirit of Zerubbabel the son of Shealtiel, governor of Judah, and the spirit of Joshua the son of Jehozadak, the high priest, and the spirit of all the remnant of the people; and they came and did work in the house of the LORD of hosts, their God, in the four and twentieth day of the month, in the sixth month, in the second year of Darius the king.

ii

In the seventh month, in the one and twentieth day of the month, came the word of the LORD by Haggai the prophet, saying:

Speak now to Zerubbabel the son of Shealtiel, governor of Judah, and to Joshua the son of Jehozadak, the high priest, and to the remnant of the people, saying, Who is left among you that saw this house in its former glory? and how do ye see it now? is it not in your eyes as nothing? Yet now be strong, O Zerubbabel, saith the LORD; and be strong, O Joshua, son of Jehozadak, the high priest; and be strong, all ye people of the land, saith the LORD, and work: for I am with you, saith the LORD of hosts, according to the word that I covenanted with you when ye came out of Egypt, and my spirit abode among you: fear ye not. For thus saith the LORD of hosts: Yet once, it is a little while, and I will shake the heavens, and the earth, and the sea, and the dry land; and I will shake all nations, and the desirable things of all nations shall come, and I will fill this house with glory, saith the LORD of hosts. The silver is mine, and the gold is mine, saith the LORD of hosts. The latter glory of this house shall be greater than the former, saith the LORD of hosts: and in this place will I give peace, saith the LORD of hosts.

iii

In the four and twentieth day of the ninth month, in the second year of Darius, came the word of the LORD by Haggai the prophet, saying:

Thus saith the LORD of hosts: Ask now the priests concerning the law, saying, If one bear holy flesh in the skirt of his garment, and with his skirt do touch bread, or pottage, or wine, or oil, or any meat, shall it become holy? And the priests answered and said, No. Then said Haggai, If one that is unclean by a dead body touch any of these, shall it be unclean? And the priests answered and said, It shall be unclean. Then answered Haggai and said, So is this people, and so is this nation before me, saith the LORD; and so is every work of their hands; and that which they offer there is unclean. And now, I pray you, consider from this day and upward, from before a stone was laid upon a stone in the temple of the LORD: through all that time, when one came to an heap of twenty measures, there were but ten; when one came to the winefat for to draw out fifty vessels, there were but twenty. I smote you with blasting and with mildew and with hail in all the work of your hands; yet ye turned not to me, saith the LORD. Consider, I pray you, from this day and upward, from the four and twentieth day of the ninth month, since the day that the foundation of the LORD's temple was laid, consider it. Is the seed yet in the barn? yea, the vine, and the fig tree, and the pomegranate, and the olive tree hath not brought forth; from this day will I bless you.

iv

And the word of the LORD came the second time unto Haggai in the four and twentieth day of the month, saying, Speak to Zerubbabel, governor of Judah, saying:

I will shake the heavens and the earth: and I will overthrow the throne of kingdoms, and I will destroy the strength of the kingdoms of the nations; and I will overthrow the chariots, and those that ride in them; and the horses and their riders shall come down, every one by the sword of his brother. In that day, saith the LORD of hosts, will I take thee, O Zerubbabel, my servant, the son of Shealtiel, saith the LORD, and will make thee as a signet: for I have chosen thee, saith the LORD of hosts.

THE BOOK

OF

ZECHARIAH

ZECHARIAH

i

The Prophet's Manifesto

*In the eighth month, in the second year of Darius,
came the word of the LORD unto Zechariah the son of
Berechiah, the son of Iddo, the prophet, saying:*

The LORD hath been sore displeased with your fathers.
Therefore say thou unto them, Thus saith the LORD of
hosts: Return unto me, saith the LORD of hosts, and I
will return unto you, saith the LORD of hosts. Be ye not
as your fathers, unto whom the former prophets cried, saying, Thus saith the LORD of hosts, Return ye now from
your evil ways, and from your evil doings: but they did
not hear, nor hearken unto me, saith the LORD. Your
fathers, where are they? and the prophets, do they live
for ever? But my words and my statutes, which I commanded my servants the prophets, did they not overtake
your fathers? and they turned and said, Like as the LORD
of hosts thought to do unto us, according to our ways, and
according to our doings, so hath he dealt with us.

ii

The Sevenfold Vision

Upon the four and twentieth day of the eleventh month, which is the month Shebat, in the second year of Darius, came the word of the LORD unto Zechariah the son of Berechiah, the son of Iddo, the prophet, saying:

The Vision Opens

I saw in the night, and behold a man riding upon a red horse, and he stood among the myrtle trees that were in the bottom; and behind him there were horses, red, sorrel, and white. Then said I, O my lord, what are these? And the angel that talked with me said unto me, I will shew thee what these be. And the man that stood among the myrtle trees answered and said, These are they whom the LORD hath sent to walk to and fro through the earth. And they answered the angel of the LORD that stood among the myrtle trees, and said, We have walked to and fro through the earth, and, behold, all the earth sitteth still, and is at rest. Then the angel of the LORD answered and said, O LORD of hosts, how long wilt thou not have mercy on Jerusalem and on the cities of Judah, against which thou hast had indignation these threescore and

ten years? And the LORD answered the angel that talked
with me with good words, even comfortable words. So
the angel that talked with me said unto me, Cry thou, saying, Thus saith the LORD of hosts: I am jealous for Jerusalem and for Zion with a great jealousy. And I am very
sore displeased with the nations that are at ease: for I
was but a little displeased, and they helped forward the
affliction. Therefore thus saith the LORD: I am returned
to Jerusalem with mercies; my house shall be built in it,
saith the LORD of hosts, and a line shall be stretched
forth over Jerusalem. Cry yet again, saying, Thus saith
the LORD of hosts: My cities shall yet overflow with
prosperity; and the LORD shall yet comfort Zion, and
shall yet choose Jerusalem.

Horns and Smiths

And I lifted up mine eyes, and saw, and behold four
horns. And I said unto the angel that talked with me,
What be these? And he answered me, These are the
horns which have scattered Judah, Israel, and Jerusalem.
And the LORD shewed me four smiths. Then said I,
What come these to do? And he spake, saying, These
are the horns which scattered Judah, so that no man did
lift up his head: but these are come to fray them, to cast

down the horns of the nations, which lifted up their horn against the land of Judah to scatter it.

2

The Measuring Line

And I lifted up mine eyes, and saw, and behold a man with a measuring line in his hand. Then said I, Whither goest thou? And he said unto me, To measure Jerusalem, to see what is the breadth thereof, and what is the length thereof. And, behold, the angel that talked with me went forth, and another angel went out to meet him, and said unto him, Run, speak to this young man, saying, Jerusalem shall be inhabited as villages without walls, by reason of the multitude of men and cattle therein. "For I, saith "the LORD, will be unto her a wall of fire round about, "and I will be the glory in the midst of her. Ho, ho, flee "from the land of the north, saith the LORD: for I have "spread you abroad as the four winds of the heaven, saith "the LORD. Ho Zion, escape, thou that dwellest with the "daughter of Babylon." For thus saith the LORD of hosts: After glory hath he sent me unto the nations which spoiled you: for he that toucheth you toucheth the apple of his eye. For, behold, I will shake mine hand over them, and they shall be a spoil to those that served them: and ye shall know that the LORD of hosts hath sent me. "Sing and rejoice, O daughter of Zion: for, lo, "I come, and I will dwell in the midst of thee, saith the "LORD. And many nations shall join themselves to the "LORD in that day, and shall be my people: and I will "dwell in the midst of thee": and thou shalt know that the LORD of hosts hath sent me unto thee. And the LORD shall inherit Judah as his portion in the holy land, and shall yet choose Jerusalem. Be silent, all flesh, before the LORD: for he is waked up out of his holy habitation.

3

The High Priest and the Adversary

And he shewed me Joshua the high priest standing before the angel of the LORD, and the Adversary standing at his right hand to be his adversary. And the LORD said unto the Adversary, The LORD rebuke thee, O Adversary; yea, the LORD that hath chosen Jerusalem rebuke thee: is not this a brand plucked out of the fire? Now Joshua was clothed with filthy garments, and stood before the angel. And he answered and spake unto those that stood before him, saying, Take the filthy garments from off him. And unto him he said, Behold, I have caused thine iniquity to pass from thee, and I will clothe thee with rich apparel. And he said, Let them set a fair diadem upon his head. So they set a fair diadem upon

his head, and clothed him with garments; and the angel
of the Lord stood by. And the angel of the Lord pro-
tested unto Joshua, saying, Thus saith the Lord of hosts:
If thou wilt walk in my ways, and if thou wilt keep my
charge, then thou also shalt judge my house, and shalt
also keep my courts, and I will give thee a place of access
among these that stand by. Hear now, O Joshua the
high priest, thou and thy fellows that sit before thee; for
they are men which are a sign: for, behold, I will bring
forth my servant the Branch. For behold, the stone that
I have set before Joshua; upon one stone are seven eyes:
behold, I will engrave the graving thereof, saith the Lord
of hosts, and I will remove the iniquity of that land in one
day. In that day, saith the Lord of hosts, shall ye call
every man his neighbour under the vine and under the
fig tree.

4

The Golden Candlestick

And the angel that talked with me came again, and
waked me, as a man that is wakened out of his sleep.
And he said unto me, What seest thou? And I said, I
have seen, and behold, a candlestick all of gold, with
its bowl upon the top of it, and its seven lamps thereon;
there are seven pipes to each of the lamps, which are upon
the top thereof: and two olive trees by it, one upon the

right side of the bowl, and the other upon the left side
thereof. And I answered and spake to the angel that
talked with me, saying, What are these, my lord? Then
the angel that talked with me answered and said unto me,
Knowest thou not what these be? And I said, No, my
lord. Then he answered and spake unto me, saying:
This is the word of the LORD unto Zerubbabel, saying,
"Not by might, nor by power, but by my spirit, saith the
"LORD of hosts. Who art thou, O great mountain?
"before Zerubbabel thou shalt become a plain: and he
"shall bring forth the head stone with shoutings of Grace,
"grace, unto it." Moreover the word of the LORD came
unto me, saying, The hands of Zerubbabel have laid the
foundation of this house; his hands shall also finish it;
and thou shalt know that the LORD of hosts hath sent me
unto you. For who hath despised the day of small things?
for they shall rejoice, and shall see the plummet in the
hand of Zerubbabel, even these seven, which are the eyes
of the LORD; they run to and fro through the whole earth.

5

The Sons of Oil

Then answered I, and said unto him, What are these
two olive trees upon the right side of the candlestick and
upon the left side thereof? And I answered the second

time, and said unto him, What be these two olive branches, which by means of the two golden spouts, empty the golden oil out of themselves? And he answered me and said, Knowest thou not what these be? And I said, No, my lord. Then said he, These are the two Sons of Oil, that stand by the Lord of the whole earth.

6

The Flying Roll

Then again I lifted up mine eyes, and saw, and behold, a flying roll. And he said unto me, What seest thou? And I answered, I see a flying roll; the length thereof is twenty cubits, and the breadth thereof ten cubits. Then said he unto me, This is the curse that goeth forth over the face of the whole land: for every one that stealeth shall be purged out on the one side according to it; and every one that sweareth shall be purged out on the other side according to it. I will cause it to go forth, saith the LORD of hosts, and it shall enter into the house of the thief, and into the house of him that sweareth falsely by my name: and it shall abide in the midst of his house, and shall consume it with the timber thereof and the stones thereof.

7

The Ephah and the Talent

Then the angel that talked with me went forth, and
said unto me, Lift up now thine eyes, and see what is this
that goeth forth. And I said, What is it? And he said,
This is the ephah that goeth forth. He said moreover,
This is their resemblance in all the land: (and behold,
there was lifted up a talent of lead:) and this is a woman
sitting in the midst of the ephah. And he said, This is
Wickedness; and he cast her down into the midst of the
ephah: and he cast the weight of lead upon the mouth
thereof. Then lifted I up mine eyes, and saw, and behold,
there came forth two women, and the wind was in their
wings: now they had wings like the wings of a stork:
and they lifted up the ephah between the earth and the
heaven. Then said I to the angel that talked with me,
Whither do these bear the ephah? And he said unto me,
To build her an house in the land of Shinar: and when it
is prepared, she shall be set there upon her own base.

The Vision Closes

And again I lifted up mine eyes, and saw, and behold,
there came four chariots out from between the two mountains; and the mountains were mountains of brass. In
the first chariot were red horses; and in the second

chariot black horses; and in the third chariot white horses; and in the fourth chariot grisled bay horses. Then I answered and said unto the angel that talked with me, What are these, my lord? And the angel answered and said unto me, These are the four winds of heaven, which go forth from standing before the Lord of all the earth. The chariot wherein are the black horses goeth forth toward the north country; and the white went forth after them; and the grisled went forth toward the south country. And the bay went forth, and sought to go that they might walk to and fro through the earth: and he said, Get you hence, walk to and fro through the earth. So they walked to and fro through the earth. Then cried he upon me, and spake unto me, saying, Behold, they that go toward the north country have quieted my spirit in the north country.

* *
*

And the word of the LORD came unto me, saying, Take of them of the captivity, even of Heldai, of Tobijah, and of Jedaiah; and come thou the same day, and go into the house of Josiah the son of Zephaniah, whither they are come from Babylon; yea, take of them silver and gold, and make crowns, and set them upon the head of Joshua the son of Jehozadak, the high priest; and speak unto him, saying, Thus speaketh the LORD of hosts, saying; Behold, the man whose name is the Branch; and he shall grow up out of his place, and he shall build the temple of the LORD: even he shall build the temple of the LORD; and he shall bear the glory, and shall sit and rule upon his throne; and he shall be a priest upon his throne: and the counsel of peace shall be between them both. And the crowns shall be to Helem, and to Tobijah, and to Jedaiah, and to Hen the son of Zephaniah, for a memorial in the temple of the LORD. And they that are far off shall come and build in the temple of the LORD, and ye shall know that the LORD of hosts hath sent me unto you. And this shall come to pass, if ye will diligently obey the voice of the LORD your God.

iii

The Inquiry on Fasting

And it came to pass in the fourth year of king Darius, that the word of the LORD came unto Zechariah in the fourth day of the ninth month, even in Chislev. Now they of Beth-el had sent Sharezer and Regem-melech, and their men, to intreat the favour of the LORD, and to speak unto the priests of the house of the LORD of hosts, and to the prophets, saying, Should I weep in the fifth month, separating myself, as I have done these so many years? Then came the word of the LORD of hosts unto me, saying:

Speak unto all the people of the land, and to the priests, saying: When ye fasted and mourned in the fifth and in the seventh month, even these seventy years, did ye at all fast unto me, even to me? And when ye eat, and when ye drink, do not ye eat for yourselves, and drink for yourselves?

2

Should ye not hear the words which the LORD hath cried by the former prophets, when Jerusalem was inhabited and in prosperity, and the cities thereof round about her, and the South and the lowland were inhabited?

(And the word of the LORD came unto Zechariah, saying,)

Thus hath the LORD of hosts spoken, saying, "Execute "true judgement, and shew mercy and compassion every "man to his brother: and oppress not the widow, nor the "fatherless, the stranger, nor the poor; and let none of "you imagine evil against his brother in your heart." But they refused to hearken, and pulled away the shoulder, and stopped their ears, that they should not hear. Yea, they made their hearts as an adamant stone, lest they should hear the law, and the words which the LORD of hosts had sent by his spirit by the hand of the former prophets: therefore came there great wrath from the LORD of hosts. And it came to pass that, as he cried, and they would not hear; so they shall cry, and I will not hear, said the LORD of hosts; but I will scatter them with a whirlwind among all the nations whom they have not known. Thus the land was desolate after them, that no man passed through nor returned: for they laid the pleasant land desolate.

3

(And the word of the LORD of hosts came to me, saying,)

"Thus saith the LORD of hosts: I am jealous for Zion "with great jealousy, and I am jealous for her with great "fury."

"Thus saith the LORD: I am returned unto Zion, and "will dwell in the midst of Jerusalem: and Jerusalem "shall be called The city of truth; and the mountain of "the LORD of hosts The holy mountain."

"Thus saith the LORD of hosts: There shall yet old "men and old women dwell in the streets of Jerusalem, "every man with his staff in his hand for very age. And "the streets of the city shall be full of boys and girls play-"ing in the streets thereof."

"Thus saith the LORD of hosts: If it be marvellous in "the eyes of the remnant of this people in those days,

"should it also be marvellous in mine eyes? saith the
"LORD of hosts."

"Thus saith the LORD of hosts: Behold, I will save my
"people from the east country, and from the west country:
"and I will bring them, and they shall dwell in the midst
"of Jerusalem; and they shall be my people, and I will
"be their God, in truth and in righteousness."

Thus saith the LORD of hosts: Let your hands be
strong, ye that hear in these days these words from the
mouth of the prophets, which were in the day that the
foundation of the house of the LORD of hosts was laid,
even the temple, that it might be built. For before those
days there was no hire for man, nor any hire for beast;
neither was there any peace to him that went out or came
in because of the adversary: for I set all men every one
against his neighbour. But now I will not be unto the
remnant of this people as in the former days, saith the
LORD of hosts. For there shall be the seed of peace;
the vine shall give her fruit, and the ground shall give her
increase, and the heavens shall give their dew; and I will
cause the remnant of this people to inherit all these things.
And it shall come to pass that, as ye were a curse among
the nations, O house of Judah and house of Israel, so will
I save you, and ye shall be a blessing: fear not, but let
your hands be strong. For thus saith the LORD of hosts:
As I thought to do evil unto you, when your fathers provoked me to wrath, saith the LORD of hosts, and I repented

not; so again have I thought in these days to do good unto Jerusalem and to the house of Judah: fear ye not. These are the things that ye shall do; Speak ye every man the truth with his neighbour; execute the judgement of truth and peace in your gates: and let none of you imagine evil in your hearts against his neighbour; and love no false oath: for all these are things that I hate, saith the LORD.

4

(And the word of the LORD of hosts came unto me, saying,)

Thus saith the LORD of hosts: The fast of the fourth month, and the fast of the fifth, and the fast of the seventh, and the fast of the tenth, shall be to the house of Judah joy and gladness, and cheerful feasts; therefore love truth and peace.

Thus saith the LORD of hosts: It shall yet come to pass that there shall come peoples, and the inhabitants of many cities: and the inhabitants of one city shall go to another, saying, Let us go speedily to intreat the favour of the LORD, and to seek the LORD of hosts: I will go also. Yea, many peoples and strong nations shall come to seek the LORD of hosts in Jerusalem, and to intreat the favour of the LORD.

Thus saith the LORD of hosts: In those days it shall

come to pass, that ten men shall take hold, out of all the languages of the nations, shall even take hold of the skirt of him that is a Jew, saying, We will go with you, for we have heard that God is with you.

Anonymous

THE KING OF PEACE

✻

*THE WITHDRAWAL OF THE DIVINE
SHEPHERD*

✻

THREE PROPHECIES OF THE SIEGE

✻

MY MESSENGER (or MALACHI)

THE KING OF PEACE

The burden of the word of the LORD upon the land of
Hadrach, and Damascus shall be its resting place: (for
the LORD hath an eye upon men and upon all the tribes
of Israel:) and Hamath also which bordereth thereon:
Tyre and Zidon, though she is very wise. And Tyre did
build herself a strong hold, and heaped up silver as the
dust, and fine gold as the mire of the streets. Behold, the
Lord will dispossess her, and he will smite her power in
the sea; and she shall be devoured with fire. Ashkelon
shall see it, and fear; Gaza also, and shall be sore pained:
and Ekron, for her expectation shall be ashamed: and
the king shall perish from Gaza, and Ashkelon shall not
be inhabited. And a bastard race shall dwell in Ashdod,
and I will cut off the pride of the Philistines. And I will
take away his blood out of his mouth, and his abominations from between his teeth; and he also shall be a remnant for our God: and he shall be as a chieftain in Judah,
and Ekron as a Jebusite. And I will encamp about mine

house as a garrison, that none pass through or return: and no oppressor shall pass through them any more: for now have I seen with mine eyes.

> Rejoice greatly, O daughter of Zion;
>> Shout, O daughter of Jerusalem:
> Behold, thy King cometh unto thee:
>> He is just, and having salvation;
> Lowly, and riding upon an ass,
>> Even upon a colt, the foal of an ass.

And I will cut off the chariot from Ephraim, and the horse from Jerusalem, and the battle bow shall be cut off; and he shall speak peace unto the nations: and his dominion shall be from sea to sea, and from the River to the ends of the earth. As for thee also, because of the blood of thy covenant I have sent forth thy prisoners out of the pit wherein is no water. Return you to the strong hold, ye prisoners of hope: even today do I declare that I will render double unto thee. For I have bent Judah for me, I have filled the bow with Ephraim; and I will stir up thy sons, O Zion, against thy sons, O Greece, and will make thee as the sword of a mighty man.

> And the LORD shall be seen over them,
>> And his arrow shall go forth as the lightning:
> And the Lord GOD shall blow the trumpet,
>> And shall go with whirlwinds of the south.

Anonymous ☙

The LORD of hosts shall defend them;
    And they shall devour, and tread down the sling
        stones;
And they shall drink, and make a noise as through
        wine:
    And they shall be filled like bowls, like the corners
        of the altar.

And the LORD their God shall save them in that day
        as the flock of his people:
    For they shall be as the stones of a crown glit-
        tering upon his land.
For how great is their goodness, and how great is
        their beauty!
    Corn shall make the young men flourish, and new
        wine the maids.

2

Ask ye of the LORD rain in the time of the latter rain,
even of the LORD that maketh lightnings; and he shall
give them showers of rain, to every one grass in the field.
For the teraphim have spoken vanity, and the diviners
have seen a lie; and the dreamers speak falsely, they comfort in vain: therefore they go their way like sheep, they
are afflicted, because there is no shepherd. Mine anger

is kindled against the shepherds, and I will punish the
he-goats: for the LORD of hosts hath visited his flock the
house of Judah, and shall make them as his goodly horse
in the battle. From him shall come forth the corner
stone, from him the nail, from him the battle bow, from
him every exactor together. And they shall be as mighty
men, treading down their enemies in the mire of the
streets in the battle; and they shall fight, because the
LORD is with them: and the riders on horses shall be
confounded. And I will strengthen the house of Judah,
and I will save the house of Joseph, and I will bring them
again, for I have mercy upon them; and they shall be as
though I had not cast them off: for I am the LORD their
God, and I will hear them. And they of Ephraim shall
be like a mighty man, and their heart shall rejoice as
through wine: yea, their children shall see it, and rejoice;
their heart shall be glad in the LORD. I will hiss for
them, and gather them; for I have redeemed them: and
they shall increase as they have increased. And though
I sow them among the peoples they shall remember me
in far countries: and they shall live with their children,
and shall return. I will bring them again also out of the
land of Egypt, and gather them out of Assyria; and I will
bring them into the land of Gilead and Lebanon; and
place shall not be found for them. And he shall pass
through the sea of affliction, and shall smite the sea of
waves, and all the depths of the Nile shall dry up: and the

Anonymous &~

pride of Assyria shall be brought down, and the sceptre
of Egypt shall depart away.   And I will strengthen them
in the LORD; and they shall walk up and down in his
name, saith the LORD.

Open thy doors, O Lebanon,
That the fire may devour thy cedars!
Howl, O fir tree, for the cedar is fallen,
Because the goodly ones are spoiled!
Howl, O ye oaks of Bashan,
For the strong forest is come down!

A voice of the howling of the shepherds!
For their glory is spoiled.
A voice of the roaring of young lions!
For the pride of Jordan is spoiled.

THE WITHDRAWAL OF THE DIVINE SHEPHERD

A THREEFOLD EMBLEM

i

The Flock of Slaughter

Thus said the LORD my God: Feed the flock of slaughter: whose buyers slay them, and hold themselves not guilty; and they that sell them say, Blessed be the LORD, for I am rich; and their shepherd pitieth them not. For I will no more pity the inhabitants of the land, saith the LORD: but, lo, I will deliver the men every one into his neighbour's hand, and into the hand of his king: and they shall smite the land, and out of their hand I will not deliver them.

So I fed the flock of slaughter: verily the most miserable of sheep!

ii

Graciousness and Union

And I took unto me two staves; the one I called Graciousness, and the other I called Union; and I fed the flock. And I cut off the three shepherds in one month; for my soul was weary of them, and their soul also loathed me. Then said I, I will not feed you: that that dieth, let it die; and that that is to be cut off, let it be cut off; and let them which are left eat every one the flesh of another. And I took my staff Graciousness, and cut it asunder, that I might break my covenant which I had made with all the peoples. And it was broken in that day: and thus the poor of the flock that gave heed unto me knew that it was the word of the LORD. And I said unto them, If ye think good, give me my hire; and if not, forbear. So they weighed for my hire thirty pieces of silver. And the LORD said unto me, Cast it unto the potter, the goodly price that I was prised at of them. And I took the thirty pieces of silver, and cast them unto the potter, in the house of the LORD. Then I cut asunder mine other staff, even Union, that I might break the brotherhood between Judah and Israel.

iii

The Foolish Shepherd

And the LORD said unto me, Take unto thee yet again the instruments of a foolish shepherd. For, lo, I will raise up a shepherd in the land, which shall not miss those that be lost, neither shall seek those that be scattered, nor heal that that is broken; neither shall he feed that which is sound, but he shall eat the flesh of the fat, and shall tear their hoofs in pieces. Woe to the worthless shepherd that leaveth the flock! the sword shall be upon his arm, and upon his right eye: his arm shall be clean dried up, and his right eye shall be utterly darkened.

THREE PROPHECIES OF THE SIEGE

i

The Fountain for the House of David

Thus saith the LORD, which stretcheth forth the heavens, and layeth the foundation of the earth, and formeth the spirit of man within him: Behold, I will make Jerusalem a cup of reeling unto all the peoples round about, and upon Judah also shall it be in the siege against Jerusalem. And it shall come to pass in that day, that I will make Jerusalem a burdensome stone for all the peoples; all that burden themselves with it shall be sore wounded; and all the nations of the earth shall be gathered together against it. In that day, saith the LORD, I will smite every horse with astonishment, and his rider with madness: and I will open mine eyes upon the house of Judah, and will smite every horse of the peoples with blindness. And the chieftains of Judah shall say in their heart, The inhabitants of Jerusalem are my strength in the LORD of hosts their God. In that day will I make the chieftains of Judah like a pan of fire among wood, and like a torch of fire among sheaves; and they shall devour all the peoples

round about, on the right hand and on the left: and Jerusalem shall yet again dwell in her own place, even in
Jerusalem.   The LORD also shall save the tents of Judah
first, that the glory of the house of David and the glory
of the inhabitants of Jerusalem be not magnified above
Judah.   In that day shall the LORD defend the inhabitants
of Jerusalem; and he that is feeble among them at that
day shall be as David; and the house of David shall be as
God, as the angel of the LORD before them.   And it shall
come to pass in that day, that I will seek to destroy all the
nations that come against Jerusalem.

And I will pour upon the house of David, and upon the
inhabitants of Jerusalem, the spirit of grace and of supplication; and they shall look unto me whom they have
pierced: and they shall mourn for him, as one mourneth
for his only son, and shall be in bitterness for him, as one
that is in bitterness for his firstborn.   In that day shall
there be a great mourning in Jerusalem, as the mourning
of Hadadrimmon in the valley of Megiddon.   And the
land shall mourn, every family apart; the family of the
house of David apart, and their wives apart; the family
of the house of Nathan apart, and their wives apart; the
family of the house of Levi apart, and their wives apart;
the family of the Shimeites apart, and their wives apart;
all the families that remain, every family apart, and their
wives apart.

In that day there shall be a fountain opened to the

house of David and to the inhabitants of Jerusalem, for sin and for uncleanness. And it shall come to pass in that day, saith the LORD of hosts, that I will cut off the names of the idols out of the land, and they shall no more be remembered. And also I will cause the prophets and the unclean spirit to pass out of the land. And it shall come to pass that, when any shall yet prophesy, then his father and his mother that begat him shall say unto him, Thou shalt not live; for thou speakest lies in the name of the LORD: and his father and his mother that begat him shall thrust him through when he prophesieth. And it shall come to pass in that day, that the prophets shall be ashamed every one of his vision, when he prophesieth; neither shall they wear a hairy mantle to deceive: but he shall say, I am no prophet, I am a tiller of the ground; for I have been made a bondman from my youth. And one shall say unto him, What are these wounds between thine arms? Then he shall answer, Those with which I was wounded in the house of my friends.

ii

The Smiting of the Shepherd and the Scattering of the Sheep

Awake, O sword, against my shepherd, and against the man that is my fellow, saith the LORD of hosts: smite the shepherd, and the sheep shall be scattered; and I will turn mine hand upon the little ones. And it shall come to pass, that in all the land, saith the LORD, two parts therein shall be cut off and die; but the third shall be left therein. And I will bring the third part through the fire, and will refine them as silver is refined, and will try them as gold is tried: they shall call on my name, and I will hear them: I will say, It is my people; and they shall say, The LORD is my God.

iii

The Judgment and the Age of Holiness

Behold, a day of the LORD cometh, when thy spoil shall be divided in the midst of thee. For I will gather all nations against Jerusalem to battle; and the city shall be taken, and the houses rifled, and the women ravished: and half of the city shall go forth into captivity. And the residue of the people shall not be cut off from the city. Then shall the LORD go forth, and fight against those nations, as when he fought in the day of battle. And his feet shall stand in that day upon the mount of Olives, which is before Jerusalem on the east, and the mount of Olives shall cleave in the midst thereof toward the east and toward the west, a very great valley; and half of the mountain shall remove toward the north, and half of it toward the south. And ye shall flee by the valley of my mountains; for the valley of the mountains shall reach unto Azel: yea, ye shall flee, like as ye fled from before the earthquake in the days of Uzziah king of Judah. And the LORD my God shall come, and all the holy ones with thee. And it shall come to pass in that day, that the light shall not be with brightness and with gloom: but it shall be one day which is known unto the LORD; not day, and not night: but it shall come to pass, that at evening time there shall be light. And it shall come to pass in that day, that living waters shall go out from Jerusalem; half of them toward the eastern sea, and half of them toward the western sea: in summer and in winter shall it be. And the LORD shall be king over all the earth: in that day shall the LORD be one, and his name one. All the land shall be turned as the Arabah, from Geba to Rimmon south of Jerusalem; and she shall be lifted up, and shall dwell in her place, from Benjamin's gate unto the place of the first gate, unto the corner gate, and from the tower of Hananel unto the king's winepresses. And men shall dwell therein, and there shall be no more curse; but Jerusalem shall dwell safely.

And this shall be the plague wherewith the LORD will smite all the peoples that have warred against Jerusalem: their flesh shall consume away while they stand upon their feet, and their eyes shall consume away in their sockets, and their tongue shall consume away in their mouth. And it shall come to pass in that day, that a great tumult from the LORD shall be among them; and they shall lay hold every one on the hand of his neighbour, and his hand shall rise up against the hand of his neighbour. And Judah also shall fight at Jerusalem; and the wealth of all the nations round about shall be gathered together, gold, and silver, and apparel, in great abundance. And so shall be the plague of the horse, of the mule, of the camel, and of the ass, and of all the beasts that shall be in those camps, as this plague. And it shall come to pass, that every one that is left of all the nations which came against Jerusalem shall go up from year to year to worship the King, the LORD of hosts, and to keep the feast of tabernacles. And it shall be, that whoso of all the families of the earth goeth not up unto Jerusalem to worship the King, the LORD of hosts, upon them there shall be no rain. And if the family of Egypt go not up, and come not, shall there not be upon them the plague, wherewith the LORD will smite the nations that go not up to keep the feast of tabernacles? This shall be the punishment of Egypt, and the punishment of all the nations that go not up to keep the feast of tabernacles.

In that day shall there be upon the bells of the horses, 𝔥𝔬𝔩𝔶 𝔲𝔫𝔱𝔬 𝔱𝔥𝔢 𝔏𝔬𝔯𝔡; and the pots in the LORD'S house shall be like the bowls before the altar. Yea, every pot in Jerusalem and in Judah shall be holy unto the LORD of

Anonymous &

hosts: and all they that sacrifice shall come and take of them, and seethe therein: and in that day there shall be no more a trafficker in the house of the LORD of hosts.

MY MESSENGER

(*MALACHI*)

.

I have loved you, saith the LORD. *Yet ye say, Wherein hast thou loved us?* Was not Esau Jacob's brother? saith the LORD: yet I loved Jacob; but Esau I hated, and made his mountains a desolation, and gave his heritage to the jackals of the wilderness. Whereas Edom saith, We are beaten down, but we will return and build the waste places; thus saith the LORD of hosts, They shall build, but I will throw down: and men shall call them The border of wickedness, and The people against whom the LORD hath indignation for ever. And your eyes shall see, and ye shall say, The LORD be magnified beyond the border of Israel.

2

A son honoureth his father, and a servant his master: if then I be a father, where is mine honour? and if I be a master, where is my fear? saith the LORD of hosts unto you, O priests, that despise my name. *And ye say, Wherein have we despised thy name?* Ye offer polluted bread upon mine altar. *And ye say, Wherein have we polluted thee?* In that ye say, The table of the LORD is contemptible. And when ye offer the blind for sacrifice, it is no evil! and when ye offer the lame and sick, it is no evil! Present it now unto thy governor; will he be pleased with thee? or will he accept thy person? saith the LORD of hosts. 'And now, I pray you, intreat the favour of God, that he may be gracious unto us : this hath been from your hand:' will he accept any because of you? saith the LORD of hosts. Oh that there were one among you that would shut the doors, that ye might not kindle fire on mine altar in vain! I have no pleasure in you, saith the LORD of hosts, neither will I accept an offering at your hand. For from the rising of the sun even unto the going down of the same my name is great among the Gentiles ; and in every place incense is offered unto my name, and a pure offering: for my name is great among the Gentiles, saith the LORD of hosts. But ye profane it, in that ye say, The table of the LORD is polluted, and the fruit thereof, even his meat, is contemptible. Ye say also, Behold, what a weariness is it! and ye have snuffed at it, saith the LORD of hosts ; and ye have brought that which was taken by violence, and the lame, and the sick; thus ye bring the offering: should I accept this of your hand? saith the LORD. But cursed be the deceiver, which hath in his flock a male, and voweth, and sacrificeth unto the Lord a blemished thing: for I am a great king, saith the

LORD of hosts, and my name is terrible among the Gentiles. And now, O ye priests, this commandment is for you. If ye will not hear, and if ye will not lay it to heart, to give glory unto my name, saith the LORD of hosts, then will I send the curse upon you, and I will curse your blessings: yea, I have cursed them already, because ye do not lay it to heart. Behold, I will rebuke the seed for your sake, and will spread dung upon your faces, even the dung of your sacrifices; and ye shall be taken away with it. And ye shall know that I have sent this commandment unto you, that my covenant might be with Levi, saith the LORD of hosts. My covenant was with him of life and peace; and I gave them to him that he might fear, and he feared me, and stood in awe of my name. The law of truth was in his mouth, and unrighteousness was not found in his lips: he walked with me in peace and uprightness, and did turn many away from iniquity. For the priest's lips should keep knowledge, and they should seek the law at his mouth: for he is the messenger of the LORD of hosts. But ye are turned aside out of the way; ye have caused many to stumble in the law; ye have corrupted the covenant of Levi, saith the LORD of hosts. Therefore have I also made you contemptible and base before all the people, according as ye have not kept my ways, but have had respect of persons in the law.

Anonymous ✃

3

Have we not all one father? hath not one God created us? why do we deal treacherously every man against his brother, profaning the covenant of our fathers? Judah hath dealt treacherously, and an abomination is committed in Israel and in Jerusalem; for Judah hath profaned the holiness of the LORD which he loveth, and hath married the daughter of a strange god. The LORD will cut off to the man that doeth this him that waketh and him that answereth, out of the tents of Jacob, and him that offereth an offering unto the LORD of hosts. And this again ye do: ye cover the altar of the LORD with tears, with weeping, and with sighing, insomuch that he regardeth not the offering any more, neither receiveth it with good will at your hand. *Yet ye say, Wherefore?* Because the LORD hath been witness between thee and the wife of thy youth, against whom thou hast dealt treacherously, though she is thy companion, and the wife of thy covenant. And not one hath done so who had a residue of the spirit. Or what? is there one that seeketh a godly seed? Therefore take heed to your spirit, and let none deal treacherously against the wife of his youth. For I hate putting away, saith the LORD, the God of Israel, and him that covereth his garment with violence, saith the LORD of hosts: therefore take heed to your spirit, that ye deal not treacherously.

4

Ye have wearied the LORD with your words. *Yet ye say, Wherein have we wearied him?* In that ye say, Every one that doeth evil is good in the sight of the LORD, and he delighteth in them; or where is the God of judgement? Behold, I send 𝔐𝔶 𝔐𝔢𝔰𝔰𝔢𝔫𝔤𝔢𝔯, and he shall prepare the way before me: and the Lord, whom ye seek, shall suddenly come to his temple; and the messenger of the covenant, whom ye delight in, behold, he cometh, saith the LORD of hosts. But who may abide the day of his coming? and who shall stand when he appeareth? for he is like a refiner's fire, and like fullers' soap: and he shall sit as a refiner and purifier of silver, and he shall purify the sons of Levi, and purge them as gold and silver; and they shall offer unto the LORD offerings in righteousness. Then shall the offering of Judah and Jerusalem be pleasant unto the LORD, as in the days of old, and as in ancient years. And I will come near to you to judgement; and I will be a swift witness against the sorcerers, and against the adulterers, and against false swearers; and against those that oppress the hireling in his wages, the widow, and the fatherless, and that turn aside the stranger from his right, and fear not me, saith the LORD of hosts. For I the LORD change not; therefore ye, O sons of Jacob, are not consumed.

5

From the days of your fathers ye have turned aside from mine ordinances, and have not kept them. Return unto me, and I will return unto you, saith the LORD of hosts. *But ye say, Wherein shall we return?* Will a man rob God? yet ye rob me. *But ye say, Wherein have we robbed thee?* In tithes and offerings. Ye are cursed with the curse; for ye rob me, even this whole nation. Bring ye the whole tithe into the storehouse, that there may be meat in mine house, and prove me now herewith, saith the LORD of hosts, if I will not open you the windows of heaven, and pour you out a blessing, that there shall not be room enough to receive it. And I will rebuke the devourer for your sakes, and he shall not destroy the fruits of your ground; neither shall your vine cast her fruit before the time in the field, saith the LORD of hosts. And all nations shall call you happy: for ye shall be a delightsome land, saith the LORD of hosts.

6

Your words have been stout against me, saith the LORD. *Yet ye say, Wherein have we spoken against thee?* Ye have said, 'It is vain to serve God: and what profit is it 'that we have kept his charge, and that we have walked 'mournfully before the LORD of hosts? And now we call 'the proud happy; yea, they that work wickedness are 'built up; yea, they tempt God and are delivered.' Then they that feared the LORD spake one with another : and the LORD hearkened, and heard, and a book of remembrance was written before him, for them that feared the LORD, and that thought upon his name. And they shall be mine, saith the LORD of hosts, in the day that I do make, even a peculiar treasure ; and I will spare them, as a man spareth his own son that serveth him. Then shall ye return and discern between the righteous and the wicked, between him that serveth God and him that serveth him not. For, behold, the day cometh, it burneth as a furnace; and all the proud, and all that work wickedness, shall be stubble: and the day that cometh shall burn them up, saith the LORD of hosts, that it shall leave them neither root nor branch. But unto you that fear my name shall the sun of righteousness arise with healing in his wings ; and ye shall go forth, and gambol as calves of the stall. And ye shall tread down the wicked; for they shall be ashes under the soles of your feet in the day that I do make, saith the LORD of hosts.

7

Remember ye the law of Moses my servant, which I commanded unto him in Horeb for all Israel, even statutes and judgements: behold, I will send you Elijah the

Anonymous ❧

𝔓𝔯𝔬𝔭𝔥𝔢𝔱 before the great and terrible day of the LORD come. And he shall turn the heart of the fathers to the children, and the heart of the children to their fathers; lest I come and smite the earth with a curse.

NOTES

It will be observed that only in exceptional cases have I given comments upon particular passages, cited by the pages on which they occur. For the most part what explanation I offer takes the form of analysis of discourses, or other divisions of prophecy; this analytic comment is distinguished to the eye by indenting, and as a rule what stands between two dashes represents a paragraph of the text.

DANIEL

Before a literary work can be correctly described it is necessary to grasp it in its unity. A difficulty in regard to this attaches to the *Book of Daniel*, from the fact that two distinct structures underlie the surface of the work, which need explaining and, as far as may be, harmonising. (1) On the one hand, the book contains, first, a series of six prophetic stories, presenting Daniel and his comrades as faithful to their religion amid Babylonian surroundings, while Daniel himself is described as miraculously endowed with power to read mysteries supernaturally manifested to others. This part of the work is told in the third person, and seems to be brought to a conclusion in the words: *So this Daniel prospered in the reign of Darius, and in the reign of Cyrus the Persian.* Then follows, as, a seventh section, an apocalypse or revelation, in which alike the supernatural manifestations and their interpretations are given to Daniel himself from without; throughout this revelation Daniel speaks in the first person. (2) On the other hand, it is to be noted that the commencement and the latter part of the book are in Hebrew, while the middle is in the Aramaic dialect. (See pages 6, 31.) The Aramaic portion commences just where (in the second story) certain Chaldeans are described as speaking *in the Syrian language;* the dialect continues, however, long past the speech so commenced, and through subsequent sections; until Hebrew is, for no obvious reason, resumed in the middle of the seventh section (the revelation), at the commencement of the second of the four visions of which this section is made up.

A simple explanation of this double structure would be to suppose that the Aramaic portion was a fragment, — a fragment in the strictest sense, commencing abruptly in the middle of a sentence; and that this was completed by a Hebrew writer, who both supplied an introduction leading up to the abrupt commencement of the fragment, and also added further visions. For both his contributions he would probably use traditional material: that there was plenty of such material attaching to the history of Daniel is clear from the stories of Daniel that are preserved in apocryphal scriptures. It will be observed that, on this supposition, both the literary types which are united in the complete *Book of Daniel* — prophetic story and apocalypse — would be within the Aramaic fragment; the Hebrew editor enlarged, but did not alter, the character of the work. He even kept up the narration in the first person, which is found in the Aramaic portion from the point where the revelation commences.*

If such a supposition be correct, it might be expected that difference of detail would be perceptible between the style or spirit of the original and the additional matter: and this is found to be the case. So far as the supplementary commencement is concerned, it amounts to no more than an explanation

---

* It will be noted that the suggestion here made is different from Meinhold's theory, which supposes only ii. 4-vi to have been the original fragment

as to who Daniel and his comrades were, and the addition of the
circumstance, entirely in keeping with what follows, that they
made a stand against defiling themselves with the king's meat.
But it is different with the three visions added to the single
vision which constituted the revelation of the Aramaic fragment:
here important differences of spirit are noticeable. (1) The
elements of the original revelation are within the limits of the
typical, and thus entirely in the spirit of emblem prophecy:
four portentous beasts, symbolising mutations of kingdoms,
contrasted with the reign of the saints. In the visions which
are added we get *particular* kingdoms, specific events. The
two-horned Ram and the He-goat are at once interpreted as
the king of Media and Persia and the king of Greece; we
read subsequently of a 'king of the north' and a 'king of the
south,' and elaborate details of their union and discord. The
whole spirit of the revelation is changed: from what has been
called the prophetic philosophy of history we pass to a very
different interest — specific prediction of the future. (2) Again,
in the fragment the machinery of vision (so to speak) is taken
for granted: *I saw in my vision by night, and behold — I
came near unto one of them that stood by, and asked him*, etc.
In the Hebrew portion great pains is taken to emphasise the
supernatural character of the visitation: it is said how the
prophet was in reality in one province while in the vision he
seemed to be in another; elaborate details are given of the
physical prostration attending the contact with the superhuman;
it is remarked how Daniel alone saw the vision, while those with
him quaked and fled but saw nothing. If the editor has kept

within the form of his original, he has enlarged from it in the spirit of the writing.

As the *Book of Daniel* is found to have a twofold structure, so the motive or purpose of the work must be pronounced twofold. If the book be taken as it stands, and the relation of its component parts examined, then the general purpose of the whole seems to be this: the six stories emphasise the character of Daniel and his God-given power to read supernatural mysteries — a power tested of course by the events — as a basis of credibility for the final revelation made to himself, much of which (it must be supposed) yet remained to be fulfilled. When, however, we read the Aramaic fragment by itself, any such underlying purpose is thrown into the background by another. The older *Book of Daniel* is, like the *Book of Esther*, a story of the Captivity. Daniel is the chief of several Judean captives who maintain their Hebrew faith and life against all the power of Babylon. They all, and especially Daniel, surpass the Chaldeans in their own boasted power of soothsaying and dream interpretation. They draw from the conquerors recognition of the superiority of the Hebrew God: at the close of one incident Nebuchadnezzar worships Daniel with oblation and sweet odours; on another occasion he makes a decree that every people, nation, and language that speak against the God of Shadrach, Meshach, and Abednego shall be cut in pieces; the dream of the tree that was cut down is told in a proclamation made by the Babylonian king to his whole empire in honour of the God who has brought such a marvel to pass. And as the stories of the Aramaic fragment picture the Hebrews in their captivity, so the vision which follows them foreshadows the period when that captivity shall end. Two distinct motives give point to the original fragment and the work in its complete form. But these distinct motives find their reconciliation in the suggestion that the complete book is addressed to an age of persecution, and that the mystic predictions of coming events form the consolation for a national distress not less signal than the Babylonian captivity.

Of the literary qualities of *Daniel* it is not necessary to speak at length. The Revelation of Daniel was the most prominent example of a long course of apocalyptic literature culminating, for the biblical reader, in the Revelation of St. John. The rest is the perfection of mystic story. It is the delight of children; but none the less its salient ideas — the stone cut out without hands striking down the mighty image, the three children braving the burning fiery furnace, Nebuchadnezzar eating grass like oxen and wet with the dew of heaven, Daniel in the den of lions, the writing on the wall — have been absorbed into the common heritage of poetic associations which makes the groundwork of literary speech.

Page 23. *And this is the writing that was inscribed.* I have followed an ancient tradition that Daniel, in solving the mystery of the writing on the wall, read *downward* instead of across. [Or better: down, up, down: that is, *boustrophedon.*] This much increases the realisability of the scene. It is plain that Daniel not only explains the enigmatical expressions, but also deciphers what the rest have failed to decipher. If this failure was due to some unknown alphabet, the interpreter must have said so, or else why is his interpretation instantly accepted? If, however, it be supposed that the mystic hand moved down, up, and down, then the writing visible at the end to the company of guests would seem to form a succession of words, which words would be unintelligible. (See page 23.) The prophet first reads the inscription the right way; and thus has a vantage ground from which to enforce its meaning.

Page 40. *But the prince of the kingdom of Persia withstood me one and twenty days.* The reference in this and similar passages is to the idea that the 'holy ones' or 'sons of God' or angels were guardian spirits of particular races or nations: Michael is named on the same page as the guardian spirit of Israel. A similar idea underlies *Psalms* lviii and lxxxii: for this, and the variation of the idea in *Job*, see note to the *Job* volume of this series, pages 146-7.

HOSEA

Hosea is perhaps the most powerful, certainly the most difficult, of the Minor Prophets. It is easy to sum up his general thought and prophetic attitude: it is extremely difficult to fol-

low him with detailed exegesis. This difficulty arises partly
from the unusual literary forms in which his writings are cast,
more from the rugged obscurity of his style, — an obscurity
which, like that of *Ecclesiastes,* is an element of power in the
impression of the whole, however much it may perplex the
interpretation of the details. The best treatment for such a
writer is to state briefly the landmarks of thought in the book,
and to leave the rest for the separate discussion of each section.

The dominant thought of Hosea is the passionate love of
Jehovah for his fallen people. If any reader is startled by the
term 'passionate' in application to God, it can only be because
the writings of this prophet are so unfamiliar: no word short of
this will do justice to the language of Hosea. The imagery he
applies to the Divine Being belongs to the strongest types of
human passion: he presents in God the burning love of the
husband for the wife of his youth who has turned unfaithful,
the yearning tenderness of an outraged parent for his wayward
child. It is passionate love again in another sense: the God of
Hosea is swayed to and fro by conflicting passions — of righteous indignation that will blot Israel out for ever, of relenting
tenderness which, in spite of all, will find a way of mercy. The
several sections of the book end, some in hopeless judgment,
others in restoration and peace.

The people of God in the *Book of Hosea* is northern Israel,
called, as if by a name of endearment, Ephraim; Judah is not
left out of view, but is referred to in a subordinate position, as a
degree less corrupt, yet included in the general prophetic denunciation. The details picture an Israel just answering to the

suggestion of the title-page: we can trace the merely material
prosperity of the reign of Jeroboam II, and the political break-
up that followed, as exhibited in rapid succession of short-lived
and weak kings, factious struggles of an Assyrian and an Egyptian party, the last stage before the fall and captivity. Stanley
calls Hosea the Jeremiah of Israel, Cheyne the prophet of the
decline and fall of the northern kingdom. Such a people
appears in this book of prophecy as wholly gangrened with corruption. Hosea sees corruption in the schism itself: by the
way in which he speaks of Israel "seeking the LORD their God
and David their king" he seems to regard the political rupture
as the embryo of a rupture with Jehovah. The seed has already
germinated in an adulteration of religious worship. Not indeed
that there is, as in the days of Elijah, an open Baal worship to
denounce; the worship in the high places is worship of Jehovah, under symbols of the calves, but the sacred rites are being
saturated with the sensual nature worship of the idolatries that
are all about. There is corruption again in the wild abandonment to luxury and dissipation, for which the prosperity of Jeroboam's reign had furnished material. Worst corruption of all,
the weakened people are coquetting with the neighbouring
powers, instead of seeking their salvation in a return to their
offended God.

Notwithstanding the obscurity of particular passages, the whole
Book of Hosea has a clear and pointed arrangement. It divides
into the usual seven sections. The opening and closing sections are masterpieces of prophetic literature, founded on the
two leading images under which Hosea conceives the relations

between Jehovah and his people. The first is the elaborate emblem prophecy of Gomer, the unfaithful wife. The concluding section is a still more elaborate dramatic presentation of the Divine Yearning—the father's yearning over his rebellious son. Three sections are simple discourses of prophetic denunciation, discourses however which at points reach rhapsodic realisation or dramatic dialogue. The discourses are separated by two sections of the prophetic 'sentences' which have been always recognised as so characteristic of Hosea. The whole is concluded by a lyrical epilogue.

   i. *GOMER: AN EMBLEM*
  ii. *Heavy Corruption and Light Repentance*
 iii. *Reaping the Whirlwind*
  iv. *Sentences*
   v. *A Harvest Prophecy*
  vi. *Sentences of Judgment*
 vii. *THE YEARNING OF GOD*

This discourse presents the prophet's relations with an unfaithful wife as an emblem of Jehovah's relations with Israel. The great question in this part of *Hosea* is whether we are to understand a literal narrative of events, or a parable, like Ezekiel's Parable of the Foundling, or of Oholah and Oholibah.*

* A still closer parallel to this second alternative would be the portion of the biblical *Zechariah* here presented as 'The Withdrawal of the Divine Shepherd' (above, page 210).

If the literal interpretation be taken, it is best to suppose (with Kirkpatrick) that Gomer became unfaithful after marriage, and that the prophet, meditating upon his unhappy lot, perceived a divine voice in the impulse which had led him to marry her. G. A. Smith calls the whole the Story of the Prodigal Wife.

Though the great majority of modern commentators with whom I should wish to agree unite in accepting the literal meaning, I find myself compelled to support the other view. The two main objections urged against this other interpretation seem to me deficient in weight. (1) It is said that if the whole be a parable we should find the name of the wife significant like the other names. This is at most a negative argument: etymology might at this distance of time fail to suggest an evil connotation of the name which usage might make clear to contemporaries. But is it certain that there is no etymological significance in the name? Cheyne says, "Gomer may plausibly be interpreted, 'perfection' (*i.e.* consummate in wickedness), and Diblaim 'cakes of figs' (*i.e.* the sweetness of sin)." To express what the parable requires — the adulterous attraction born of excessive luxury — what can be better than 'Perfection daughter of Fig-cake,' more especially in view of the passage (page 54): *as the LORD loveth the children of Israel, though they turn unto other gods, and love cakes of raisins?* (2) How, it is asked, could the prophet think of applying the idea of wedlock to the relation between God and his people except by some such experience? But this idea, so common in later prophets like Ezekiel, must have a commencement in some one mind: it is not for us to say how such ideas should be first inspired. On

the other hand, the whole drift of the detailed language favours
the idea that we are reading a parable: the application entirely
overweights the personal details. It is moreover self-contained,
as a parabolic discourse would be: no hint of such an experience
in the prophet's life appears in subsequent parts of the book.
Again, the discourse is in pendulum form: are we to suppose
that with the change to hope in the second paragraph the
actual names of the prophet's children are to be changed?
[The analogy of Isaiah's children and their significant names
breaks down in this respect.] In spite of the pathetic character of the literal interpretation, woven by Plumptre into a
beautiful poem, the indications seem to me strongly in favour
of understanding a parable.

The discourse is in pendulum form: successive paragraphs
alternate between judgment and hope of restoration.

 1. Israel's backsliding is presented under the emblem of
the adulterous wife: the children of the adulterous wife
symbolise successive stages of divorce from God. — Emblem reversed: a glorious restoration. — The original emblem resumed, and carried out to its furthest details. — The
reverse of the emblem expanded: allurement to repentance,
until the symbols of sin (*Joshua* vii. 24) become signs of
hope, and the mutual intercourse is restored of a praying
Jezreel and a God answering with blessings of natuie.

 2. A further application of the emblem: instead of allurement, forcing to repentance.

ii. A prophetic discourse, culminating in dramatic dialogue:

Heavy Corruption and Light Repentance. The paragraph divisions are only faintly marked.

Utter corruption and utter distress. — No place for mutual recriminations: alike are priest, prophet, and the nation which is the mother of them all. — They are left to their transgressions, the triple chain of indulgence, folly, idolatry. — At least let Judah hold back: Ephraim is committed, already caught in the swirl of judgment. — Priests and kings [the natural refuge of the people] are but a fresh snare: everything waits but for the new moon of judgment. — Cries of judgment begun: Ephraim is crushed.   [The discourse becomes dramatic.]   God will wait for affliction to do its work — and accordingly Ephraim speaks in tones of penitence. — But how trust such transitory penitence? Israel is hopelessly defiled, and there is a harvest for Judah to reap.

iii. Another prophetic discourse, realistic at one point: Reaping the Whirlwind.

When the Lord would heal, corruption appears in its full heat (see below). Signs of decay visible, but Ephraim will not see them. — Or if he sees, he goes to the wrong source for healing. — Sound the trump of judgment: now they repent too late.

Page 60. *They are as an oven heated by the baker*, etc. The imagery of the oven running through this paragraph rests on the idea that when once the oven is heated to its full heat the baker may leave it all night; it will do its work unattended. So corruption has reached the point where it will do its deadly

work of itself. — *Ephraim is a cake not turned:* baking sup-
plies one more image: the nation hurries from one alliance to
another before the first is fully formed.

Page 61. *He hath cast off thy calf, O Samaria:* in the
numerous references to the calves it must be remembered that
these were not rival gods to Jehovah, but compromises between
the worship of Jehovah and the idolatries of the neighbouring
peoples, consisting in the representation of God by a visible
symbol.

iv. This section is a string of disconnected prophetic 'sentences.' From the time of St. Jerome downwards the 'senten-
tious' style of Hosea has been noted. But such groups of
sentences are found in other prophets (compare the *Isaiah* volume, page 233: *Jeremiah* volume, page 221). Each sentence
will have some epigrammatic point: often this is obvious, sometimes it is difficult to state.

He hath no standing corn, etc. This has an epigrammatic form of which Hosea is fond: reserves of hope suc-
cessively frustrated. No blade: if there be blade, no
fruit: if there be fruit, it shall be for strangers. Compare
the third sentence of page 65 and the second sentence of
page 66. — *Israel is swallowed up,* etc.: they have spent in
buying alliances all that makes them worth bidding for. —
Like a wild ass alone: an obstinate beast that has shaken
off guidance. — *Though they hire among the nations, now
will I gather them:* the *gather* is antithetical to the idea of
dispersion implied in *among the nations:* the scattering of
their bribes shall make them feel the pinch of contracted

resources. — *Ephraim hath multiplied altars — to sin*, etc.
I have followed the felicitous punctuation of G. A. Smith.
The altars multiplied only for purposes of sin shall in the hour
of need serve only for sin, not for repentance and forgiveness.

v. A brief prophetic discourse, inspired by the sight of
harvest festivals, which, though nominally for the worship of
Jehovah, were rapidly assimilating themselves to the sensuous
and exciting orgies of idolatrous nature worship.

The conversion of harvest joy into an excited heathen
orgy [*exultation*] is as bad as the substitution of hired har-
lotry for the service of a faithful wife. The judgment will
be realised in an exile which takes away all feasts of Jehovah, and leaves no use for bread but to satisfy hunger.

vi. Another string of epigrammatic sentences : more particu-
larly threatening a judgment to come.

The prophet is a fool, etc. : God has withdrawn his spirit,
leaving prophecy no more than what its outward form
appears, mere raving. — *Ephraim was a watchman*, etc. :
once, the mountains of Ephraim were the watch-towers of
Jehovah (*Jeremiah* xxxi. 6), now his prophets are encoun-
tered with treachery and hostility. — *As in the days of
Gibeah : Judges*, chapter xix : all the life of northern Israel
is of a piece with the original scandal. Compare the third
sentence of page 67. — *I found Israel like grapes in the
wilderness :* the disappointment of watching the first promise of spring change into rotten fruit. — *Give them, O
LORD : what wilt thou give ?* The speaker sets out to in-
voke a blessing, and breaks off with the reflection that the

greatest blessing for Israel now would be no more children to suffer in the judgment. — *They speak vain words, swearing falsely in making covenants:* their covenants with the nations are so much perjury against Jehovah. — *When they are yoked to their two transgressions:* apparently, their revolt against God and Judah (so page 55: *seek the LORD their God and David their king*). — *Ephraim is an heifer that is taught:* a contrast between the pleasant task of treading the corn and the laborious task of drawing the plough. — *As Shalman spoiled Beth-arbel:* nothing is known of this allusion.

vii

This is an elaborate dramatic presentation of the Divine Father yearning over his rebellious Ephraim (Judah being occasionally included with Ephraim). It is drama of a peculiar kind: the greater part of it is alternating monologue, the Divine Being represented as swaying in alternate moods, between tender reminiscences of Israel's youth and his own loving mercies, and outbursts of righteous indignation and threatening. (Compare the *Isaiah* volume, pages 243, 244: in that case, however, there are two parties present to be alternately addressed.) At the end Repentant Israel or Ephraim enters into the drama, and monologue changes to dialogue. When once the principle is caught, and the paragraphs arranged, further analysis is unnecessary: two passages of some difficulty are explained in their place.

Page 68. *As they* [*e.g.* prophets] *called them* [the people], *so they* [the people] *went from them* [the prophets].

Page 69. *They shall walk after the LORD, who shall roar like a lion:* the context shows this means a lion roaring to call his young ones.

Page 70. *In the womb he took his brother by the heel,* etc. This and the similar verse passage on the following page are of recognised difficulty, which has led some commentators to proclaim them spurious, or out of place. In the arrangement of alternating monologue here adopted they fall into their places as part of the tender reminiscences of Deity. The pronouns in the latter part of this first passage suggest a quotation supposed to be made by God from some source where Israel is speaking of himself: *He* [Jehovah] *found him* [Israel] *at Beth-el, and there he* [Jehovah] *spake with us* [Israel]. I believe the whole that I have printed as six lines of verse to be a quotation from prophetic hymns of Israelitish history; I have argued at length for the existence of such hymns and for quotations from them in *Ecclesiasticus* (see that volume, pages 175–182). This passage and that on the following page are entirely in keeping with the marked character of those couplet hymns; and the theory of quotation explains the abrupt introduction of the passage, which all commentators note. The connection with the general argument is clear: reminiscences of youthful Israel's power with God, of God's promises to him at Beth-el: *therefore,* cries God, *turn thou,* etc. — *I will yet again make thee to dwell in tents,* etc.: Cheyne aptly compares (page 53), *I will allure her, and bring her into the wilderness,* thus making the words a threat, but a threat with a tinge of promise.

Page 71. *And Jacob fled into the field of Aram,* etc.: see previous note. The reminiscences are continued: how youthful Israel endured exile and service rather than enter into adulterating intercourse with the people of the land (*Genesis*, chapter xxviii. 1); how God on his part granted a wonder-working prophet to deliver Israel from Egypt.

Page 74. *Who is wise*, etc.: an epilogue to the whole book.

JOEL

The whole *Book of Joel* is a single piece of prophetic literature. It is not a discourse, or series of discourses, but a continuous dramatic presentation.

A Rhapsody of the Locust Plague

(For the 'rhapsody,' or spiritual drama, see *Isaiah* volume, pages vii–xii). Its subject is the regular prophetic idea of the Day of the Lord, with its twofold conception of judgment: (1) judgment upon God's people, in this case converted by penitence into purification; and (2) final judgment between the purified people and the hostile nations. Its outer form rests upon two ideas: (1) a locust plague, possibly real, idealised into mystic forces of destruction; and (2) similarly, a real place, the Valley of Jehoshaphat [= 'Jehovah judges'] idealised into a scene of final contest between the hosts of God and the hosts of Evil. The seven acts or 'visions' into which the rhapsody divides are successive in time and continuous.

 i. *The Land Desolate and Mourning*
 ii. *The Judgment advancing*

iii. Repentance at the Last Moment
iv. Relief and Restoration
v. Afterward
vi. Advance to the Valley of Decision
vii. The Holy Mountain and Eternal Peace

i. Dramatic picture of the Land mourning under a great Desolation. [This is brought out, as in oratorio form, by choruses of Old Men, Revellers, Priests, Husbandmen, lamenting to one another (in free verse) over the destruction special to each: as a climax, the Whole People (in recitative prose) summon an assembly, and (in stanza verse) present their supplication.] — **ii.** In vain: the mystic judgment advances to its climax. [This is brought out by verse passages presenting an objective picture of what is seen and heard, alternating with passages of recitative prose which add fresh terrors by seeking to analyse what is seen.] — **iii.** A surprise: when the dreaded Voice of the Lord sounds it is a call to repentance; motions of repentance stir among the people, and culminate in a supplication of the Whole People, led by the Priests. — **iv.** The turning-point is conveyed by a single clause of direct statement (for similar breaks in dramatic form, compare the *Isaiah* volume, pages 106, 107, 189). Then [in monologue of God] is brought out the removal of the mystic foe,* and the restoration of all that had been destroyed. — **v.** The next stage

---

* Called *northern army*, because the north is regularly the quarter from which judgment is looked for in prophetic literature; compare *Job*, chapter xxxvii. 22, and note on page 175 of that volume.

[still by monologue of Deity] brings out subsequent spiritualisation of God's people, and preparation for contest with the hostile nations. — **vi.** The sixth stage [in dramatic dialogue] presents the advance of the nations and the hosts of God to the conflict in the 'Valley of Decision.' The climax [described by 'the Prophetic Spectator'] is all earthquake and darkness. — **vii.** Darkness has rolled away and discloses [by Divine monologue] the Holy Mountain and the Eternal Peace of God's people.

AMOS

The *Book of Amos* as here arranged is made up of (1) a single prophetic 'sentence.' and (2) an elaborate prophecy of the type I have proposed to call 'rhapsody.' (*Isaiah* volume, pages vii–xii.)

Oracle of the Earthquake

These four lines might possibly be included in the composition that follows, as an introductory note of judgment: in that connection however they have not much relevancy or definite point. The main criterion is the question whether verse 1 is (*a*) a title-page to the whole book, as in the case of *Hosea* and *Joel*, or (*b*) a date of a particular prophecy, of the kind found in *Haggai* and *Zechariah*. The words *two years before the earthquake* seem to me decisive. There is no example of so specific a date for a general prophecy. But to the brief oracle the date gives special point: Amos, an obscure herdsman, outside prophetic circles altogether, rises to prominence by his *prediction,* two years beforehand, of a famous convulsion of nature, — 'the earthquake in the days of Uzziah' (*Zechariah,* chapter xiv. 5); this is the starting-point of a prophetic career.

The first two lines are a general prophetic formula of judgment (compare *Joel,* chapter iii. 16; *Jeremiah* xxv. 30; and imagery of *Psalm* lxxvi. 2, 4, taking the marginal readings of R.V.); the last two suggest a convulsion spreading from Jerusalem as centre to the outskirts of heath or mountain.

A Rhapsody of the Judgment to come

As regards its subject-matter this prophecy seems to be generated by a state of national life amounting to a conflict between morals and religion: Israel appears indifferent to elementary morality in proud reliance on its position as Jehovah's peculiar people. The message of Amos is that this basis of their trust will bring them the heavier judgment; it comes as a startling prophetical novelty, generating a violent antagonism to prophecy in general, the reflection of which is one of the characteristic features of the book. The picture incidentally presented is of formal worship (of the calves in Beth-aven) side by side with abandonment to luxury, avarice, oppression. The 'Judgment to come,' as usual in prophecy, appears at the last to be a sifting: none of the true corn shall perish, and the end will be glorious restoration.

The literary form is a rhapsody, presenting the coming judgment on Israel, not (like that of Joel) as a continuous dramatic movement, but (compare the *Isaiah* volume, pages x, 242) in a series of stages making a logical rather than a temporal sequence. First, by a rhetorical figure of surprise, Israel is included among the doomed nations; then the corruption is denounced as ripe for judgment; finally the judgment is in vision seen to advance by steps.

Structural elaboration makes a greater part of the total literary effect in *Amos* than in any other writer. Three structural features may be noted. One may be called the Parallel Climax structure: a series of parallel sentences (or stanzas) as a basis for one more parallel of climax. (Marked examples are Vision i, and the parenthetic passages [here printed in italics] of pages 99 and 101.) The structure of Visions ii and iii presents a less formal example of Parallels with Climax; and the number seven prevails throughout. (See analysis below.)

The third structural peculiarity is less obvious, but is very important for clear exegesis. It may be termed the Parenthetic Preface, or Prefatory Interruption. I have already noted as a feature in the style of Isaiah (see that volume, page 213) the tendency to place a prefatory explanation after or in the middle of what it prefaces or explains: such passages may be called 'prefatory' because there is a change from the message to matters personal to the messenger, such as a modern writer would deal with in his preface. With the general tendency of Amos to regularity of form, such interruptions become a structural element of the whole prophecy: I have felt justified in distinguishing them by italic type and the parenthetic form. We thus get a complex structure made up of a sustained denunciation of sin and threatening of judgment interrupted by parenthetic appeals to the opponents of prophecy: such opposition being partly open antagonism, and partly the ignoring of divine warnings by those who are absorbed in empty ritual or selfish pursuits. There are no less than six repetitions of this complex structure. — (*a*) In Vision ii, as soon as the first note of judgment has been sounded, the prophet breaks off (page 99) to work out, in a progression of seven clauses, the thought, Who that has received a prophetic message can fail to prophesy? — (*b*) Then three proclamations of judgment are uttered, and the speaker again breaks off in a protest (sevenfold in structure) against those who trust to ritual and are blind to clear signs of doom (page 101). — (*c*) The fourth section is a wail over fallen Israel: it is interrupted by snatches of appeal to the same opponents. This last case is less clear than the others, but seems clear enough. The first clause (see page 104) might be read as part of the denunciation; the second and third (page 105) are certainly better understood as citations of objections. Moreover, the general drift of the argument points the same way: the *Forasmuch therefore*, *Seek good*, *Therefore thus saith the LORD*, are replies to the objections involved in the supposed interruptions. — (*d*) In Vision iii we have advancing stages of judgment and the Divine Being speaking doom: just where judgment has been advanced to the point from which there is no retreat we get (page 109) the interrupting notice of open conflict between prophecy and authority. Here no doubt an historic incident is reflected: it appears at this point, either because in the oral ministry upon which the rhapsody is founded the incident took place where this particular emblem

of judgment had been spoken (the *then* would in this view
be temporal), or because this is its logical connection with
the theme (*then* causal). — (*e*) Section 4 of this Vision gives
a specially clear case (page 110): the Divine speech in the
first person is interrupted and resumed: the interruption is
the prophet's appeal, *Hear this, O ye that*, etc. — (*f*) Similarly
in the next section the Divine speaker brings out a further
stage of judgment, and the prophet resumes his interrupting
appeal, *For the LORD*, etc. (page 112): the two appeals of
the prophet being further bound together by the repeated
image of the inundating River. — Each example must stand
on its merits: but the case becomes all the clearer when the
whole argument and succession of interruptions are considered
together.   [See analysis below.]

> *i.   Israel among the Doomed Nations*
> *ii.   Corruption ripe for Judgment*
> *iii.   Vision of Judgment*

A series of nations denounced and threatened in parallel
stanzas: as a climax of surprise comes a final stanza (parallel,
but freer in detail) denouncing Judah and Israel.   [The stanzas
are compounded of rhythmical formulæ only varied by the names
(expressing the sin and the doom) and recitative prose (expressing actual offences and details of punishment).]

ii

Denunciation (in sevenfold structure) of Corruption ripe for Judgment — with parenthetic interruptions of Appeals to Opponents of prophecy.

Introduction: Central idea of the whole rhapsody: Because Israel is God's chosen nation, therefore it shall be visited with judgment.

Appeal (with sevenfold structure) to Opponents: The inevitableness of prophecy. [Above, page 252.]

1, 2, 3 (in Proclamation form: 'Hear ye'): Three evils denounced: luxury with oppression — empty ritual with oppression — feminine luxury with oppression.

Appeal (in sevenfold structure) to Opponents: Trusting to elaborate ritual and ignoring plain judgments.

4 (in Wail form): Israel fallen to rise no more! Seek the Lord if it be not too late!

Snatches of parenthetic appeal to Opponents: hatred of open reproof — prudential silence — weak trust that all may turn out well. [See above, page 252 (c).]

5 (in Woe form): Desiring the 'Day of the Lord' and not seeing that it will be against them.

6 (in Woe form): Putting off the evil day by those who shall be the first to suffer.

7 (the irrevocable Oath of Deity): Destruction shall be utter: Jacob an abhorrence.

iii

Vision of Judgment Advancing upon Israel (in seven emblematic stages) — with parenthetic interruptions of Appeals to Opponents of prophecy.

1, 2: Vision Emblems of Locusts, Fire: stages of judgment threatening, yet restrained in its course.

3: Vision Emblem of the Plumbline: * the exact point at which safety is lost.

Parenthetic Protest: Open conflict between prophecy and (royal and priestly) authority. [See above, page 252 (d).]

4: Vision Emblem of Summer Fruit: Israel ripe for the judgment.

The Divine speech interrupted by Appeal to Opponents, in their avarice impatient of sacred festivals while the inundation of judgment is at hand.

Divine speech continued: A material and spiritual famine, the strongest [youths, etc.] to fall first.

5: Vision Emblem of Smiting the chapiters: the Judgment begun. (The imagery of the bowing wall has developed to actual pulling down.)

Preceding Appeal to Opponents continued: It is Jehovah who brings this inundation of judgment.

* Compare the imagery of the bowing wall in *Isaiah* chapter xxx. 13, and *Psalm* lxii. 3. — The plumbline is the symbol of exactness in building operations. Thus in *Zechariah*, chapter iv. 10; the temple built without flaw — *Isaiah* xxviii. 17: all outside the exact line of righteousness shall perish — *II Kings* xxi. 13: Jerusalem shall suffer exactly as Samaria.

6: Emblem or Image of the Ethiopians, etc.: The Judgment consummated: Israel on a par with the heathen peoples. — Turning point * of Judgment. It shall be a sifting, no true corn shall perish.

7: Thus Final Vision of Restored Israel. [Emblematic form dropped.]

OBADIAH

This is the briefest of the prophetic books. A calamity falling upon Israel has been aggravated by the malignant rejoicing of her neighbour foe, Edom. Israel is comforted in the thought of a future in which Edom will suffer judgment in her turn, and the kingdom will be the Lord's.

The prophecy is in the common 'doom form' [*Isaiah* volume, page 215]: a Divine speech of doom, with lyric celebration of the theme. (In the lyric portion the double quotation marks indicate the *tidings from the LORD*. The ambassador's message does not extend beyond line 3. The rest is exultation over the coming destruction.)

JONAH

This is in literary form a prophetic story, like the Story of Elijah in *Kings*, or the earlier part of the *Book of Daniel*. Its interpretation must therefore be based upon the action of the prophet, what he fails to do as well as what he does. It falls into three sections.

* Anticipated at the beginning of ii: the shepherd rescuing fragments.

   i.   *The Flight to Tarshish*
  ii.   *Jonah's Prayer*
 iii.   *The Preaching at Nineveh*

i, iii. The first section rests upon the old conception of deity as a local power [compare *I Kings*, chapter xx. 23]. Jonah to escape an unwelcome commission flees to the far west: the storm that overtakes him reminds him that Jehovah's *power* extends beyond the holy land. — Similarly in **iii** it is brought home to him how the *mercy* of Jehovah extends beyond the chosen nation. Jonah's preaching awakens a repentance which averts the judgment on Nineveh. Jonah's feeling must not be understood as sullenness; nor does he need to be informed of the mercy of God, for he expressly makes this the basis of his former evasion of the ministry to Nineveh. But he is possessed with righteous indignation at Jehovah's extending this mercy outside his own people. God deals with this mood by enlisting his sympathy, first with a tender and beautiful thing of nature, and then with the mass of humanity and dumb nature represented in Nineveh.

    ii. Between these comes Jonah's Prayer or Thanksgiving at his escape from the sea [compare such Songs of Thanksgiving as *Psalm* xviii]. The reference to the *great fish* prepared to swallow Jonah is in literary form a footnote exegetical of the expression in the song, *Out of the belly of hell;* similarly the vomiting out Jonah is a footnote attached to the last line. These particular footnotes have every appearance of being a gloss or later addition. They are absolutely incompatible with

the words of the prayer itself, which distinctly celebrate a deliverance from immersion in the sea : compare *The deep was round
about me ; the weeds were wrapped about my head,* etc.

MICAH

This book is made up of an elaborate prophetic discourse followed by two prophecies in dramatic form.

The spirit of the whole has been felicitously described by
Mr. Findlay as uniting the pessimism of Amos and Hosea with
the Messianic optimism of the earlier Zechariah [our *Zechariah* chapter ix, etc.]. We have the age of Isaiah viewed, not
from the standpoint of the capital and the political leaders, but
from that of the country and humbler classes. The first discourse attacks social corruption and the delusive promises of
false prophets, insisting upon a purging judgment to precede
the glorious restoration. The last prophecies present the eve
of this judgment; the corrupt in their despair, and the faithful
[the 'man of wisdom'] to whom the judgment comes as deliverance, are brought into dramatic contrast.

   i.   *A Discourse of Judgment and Salvation*
   ii. *The LORD'S Controversy before the Mountains*
  iii. *The LORD'S Cry and the Man of Wisdom*

This is an elaborate Discourse of Judgment and Salvation,
with the usual sevenfold structure : the middle section being a

parenthetic protest [compare *Amos*] against the opponents of faithful prophecy.

1. A Threat of Judgment upon the sin of Israel. — 2. Rhapsodical realisation of the judgment falling on the land.* — 3. Special denunciation of social oppression. — 4. Here the prophet breaks off to attack those who would restrain his plain-speaking prophecy in the interest of oppressing rulers. He imitates the glowing promises of the popular prophets. Judgment shall descend on the oppressing rulers, and a night of no vision on the false prophets. But he is strengthened by God to declare the sin of Israel. [For the difficulties of this section see below.] — 5. Denunciation is resumed of the national corruption which will destroy Zion and Jerusalem. — 6. But then will come a restoration in which Zion will be exalted, and the nations will flow to her. — 7. The final section is an appeal, on the basis of what precedes, for hopefulness under trouble. Three pictures follow of trouble and relief: there is the anguish of exile, even as far as distant Babylon, and yet the rescue comes — again, nations are assembled against Zion, only as sheaves are brought to the threshing floor to be trodden — yet again, trooping enemies are about to strike the final blow, but One from little Bethlehem becomes a mighty power against the Assyrian, and the diminished nation is as irresistible as the dew, as mighty as the lion: all is purity and salvation.

* The effect depends partly on paranomasias, which the R. V. for the most part passes over.

Page 134. *I will surely assemble, O Jacob, all of thee.* In
this difficult passage I have followed Ewald's view that we
have here a mocking specimen of the promises of the flattering
prophets. The objections urged against this interpretation are
two: (1) the passage is too much in the style of the genuine
prophecy to be a mere citation of what is false prophecy;
(2) in particular, *the remnant of Israel* is the last phrase such
a false prophet would use. But (1) Micah's objection is not
to the glorious promises of his rivals, but to their putting these
forth without the condition precedent of judgment on sin.
(2) The word *remnant* need not have the special association
which belongs to prophecy nearer the overthrow of Judah:
it seems to be regularly applied to a race scattered in small
numbers in the midst of another race [*Joshua* chapter xxiii. 12;
II Samuel xxi. 2]. The false prophets thus declare that all
Israel, down to the remotest exiles carried captive in war, will
be assembled again for Israel's victory; whereas Micah declares
(in section 7) that only the remains of the people left after the
judgment has destroyed the rest will share in the glory. In
favour of the arrangement I have adopted is the general cohe-
rency of section 4; and especially the words, *And I said, Hear,
I pray you,* which are just suited for the words of one resuming
after quoting an adversary.

ii

This exquisite dramatic morsel puts in forensic form Jehovah's
attitude of controversy against his sinful people. He himself
arraigns: Balaam is cited as the great witness from without as

to Jehovah's goodness to Israel. — The defendant People tremble
to appear. — The Mountains as judges pronounce the foundation
truths of judgment.

iii

This dramatic presentation of judgment and salvation announces itself in its title [*The voice of the LORD crieth unto the
city*, etc.] as addressed to the City; and prepares us to expect
the Man of Wisdom [the faithful in the midst of the wicked] as
an addition to the *dramatis personæ.*   [Similar explanatory
titles are found in the *Isaiah* volume, pages 106 and 107; but
there only for portions of the drama.]

The Lord announces the rod of judgment on a corruption
ripe for it. — The sinful People speak their despair, awak-
ing to their corruption too late. — But the Man of Wisdom
receives with hopefulness this judgment which treads down
his oppressing foe. — The city being thus purified shall be
built up, and the exiles shall flock to it. But in the land
outside desolation shall still punish sin. — The Man of
Wisdom intercedes for those of the flock that are scattered
through the wilds of the land. — The Lord responds with
a deliverance as complete as that from Egypt. — The Man
of Wisdom exults at the glorious deliverance, and cele-
brates the pardoning God.

NAHUM

This splendid prophetic celebration of the Doom of Nineveh
is best classified as a 'rhapsodic discourse.' It has a general

resemblance to the 'doom form' [*Isaiah* volume, page 231], especially Jeremiah's Doom of Babylon [pages 195, 229 of that
volume], but is more varied in its parts.

1, 2. The first two sections are prophetic discourse in
pendulum form, the paragraphs swaying between the ideas
of judgment and mercy. — 3. Doom form: divine tidings
of deliverance alternating with lyric presentation of the
overthrow of Nineveh. — 4. Brief lyric meditation on Nineveh desolate. — 5. Doom form resumed: divine word of
judgment alternating with lyric presentation of the city in
its guilt. — 6. Taunt Song [compare Isaiah's Doom of
Babylon, page 52]. — 7. Brief lyric meditation on Nineveh
desolate.

HABAKKUK

This book of prophecy is here presented as a single literary
composition which may be entitled

A Rhapsody of the Chaldeans

The historical situation needs no further defining than the
recognition on the political horizon of the Chaldeans as a world
power trampling down the nations. To the pious Israelite the
first suggestion this brings is of a power for judgment on the
unpunished sin around him. But the reflecting prophet sees a
further mystery: how can a righteous God use an impious conqueror for the punishment of sin less wicked than his own?
The divinely given solution of this problem is the same thought

which Jeremiah expresses [page 198 of that volume] by calling Babylon the 'hammer' of God, an instrument of providence for the destruction of evil, to be itself destroyed when its work is done.   This is the whole thought: the rest is literary setting.

The literary form is a perfect type of the 'rhapsody.' The essential meaning of this [*Isaiah* volume, pages vii–xii] is dramatic realisation by means which include but go beyond dramatic form.   Thus in the present case we have a providential mystery developed in dramatic dialogue; for the solution of the mystery dramatic dialogue breaks into the half lyric doom form; while the climax realises the situation in the full lyric form of an ode of Jehovah come to Judgment.   Besides variety of form we thus get an intensifying dramatic movement, from dim statement of a mystery to present realisation of its solution. The working out of this is best conveyed by detailed analysis.

> *i.   The Mystery*
> *ii.   The Solution*
> *iii.   Jehovah come to Judgment*

-

The Prophet, in dialogue with God, touches the mystery of sin unpunished and judgment withheld. — God announces a marvel: the Chaldeans as a conquering power, godless and irresistible. — The Prophet finds his mystery intensified by this answer: how can righteousness use godlessness as an instrument to punish evil that is less than its own?

ii

This full statement of the problem is emphasised by the Prophet's retiring to his watchtower [compare in the *Isaiah* volume note to IV. x on page 234] to await the Divine answer. — This solution is conveyed under the gradually elaborated image of intoxication: the haughty bearing of the Chaldean is no more than the reeling of the drunkard that goes before his fall. This coming fall is suddenly presented in the Doom or Taunt Song of the delivered peoples.

Doom of the Chaldeans [in five lyric woes alternating with Divine word of denunciation: compare *Isaiah* volume, page 231].

The first four stanzas express the overthrow of the haughty Chaldeans under four different images. — 1. This unchecked career of the conqueror is a rolling up of usury: the exactor shall come. — 2. It is building a house of refuge from evil, only to find shame built into wall and beam. — 3. It is building a city by iniquity only to make a bigger bonfire to blaze abroad the avenging God. — 4. It is making a neighbour drunk and enjoying his shame only to receive the drink of shame from God. — 5. The last woe is addressed to the foundation of all: trusting in dumb idols, whereas the living Jehovah is the World's Teacher.

iii

A Vision Ode of Jehovah come to Judgment. The structure of the ode is a prelude and a postlude embodying the feelings of the Prophet as he beholds, while the body of the ode con-

tains the vision itself. [Compare the structure of *Psalm* xxix.]
The body of the ode consists of

> *Strophe :* All nature convulsed with advancing Deity.
>
> *Antistrophe :* Is it against nature that this advance is
> directed?
>
> *Epode :* Nay, it is for the salvation of his people that God
> comes. [Compare *Psalm* cxiv.]

[Strophe and antistrophe, each sixteen lines; epode, eight lines;
prelude, four lines; postlude, sixteen lines.]

Pages 162–5. *I have heard the report of thee and am afraid.
. . . I heard, and . . . my lips quivered at the voice.* The
report, voice, refer to the voice speaking what makes the body
of the ode. What exactly is this voice? Not (*a*) that of God,
or the Celestial Hosts, or such voices as speak the passages of
celebration in doom songs, because of the line, *They came as
a whirlwind to scatter me.* (*b*) Nor is the ode spoken by the
congregation of Israel (so Farrar), which would make actuality
and not vision, and leave no place for the uncertainty of the
postlude. (*c*) The voice seems to be that of Israel in vision.
This makes possible the mixed feelings of the postlude. The
intervention of Deity is only in vision, yet thus made so realisti-
cally certain that the Prophet, in the postlude, trembles with
faith: that he should feel at rest waiting for the invading
Chaldean [*when he that shall invade . . . cometh up,* etc.]: at
rest, because, *though the fig tree shall not blossom,* etc., the
Prophet [through this vision] can exult in his God. — *Revive
thy work in the midst of the years :* a reference to the *though it*

tarry wait for it of ii : the Prophet prays God to intervene before it be too late.

Page 162, footnote. *Set to Shigionoth :* A musical direction, the meaning of which is lost.

ZEPHANIAH

This is the simplest and most typical example of the 'doom form' of prophecy, presenting the familiar topic, the Day of the Lord, in a Divine word of denunciation and threatening [here presented as prose] interrupted at intervals by lyric passages seconding, celebrating, or otherwise dwelling upon successive points in the speech of Deity. [Compare the *Isaiah* volume, page 215.] The prose passages are in the first person, and may be read together as a unity apart from the interrupting lyrics.

The whole is continuous, but as regards subject-matter falls into three natural divisions.

    1. Judgment beginning at Jerusalem and sweeping over the different quarters of the city (The Mortar, etc.).— 2. Judgment spreading outside to the nations, from the Philistines to Nineveh as a climax.— 3. Beyond the judgment a restoration : the nations fearing Jehovah, Israel with its restored exiles a blessing among the peoples.

HAGGAI and ZECHARIAH

It is natural to consider Haggai and Zechariah * together. They are fellow workers in the great work of rebuilding the

---

* That is, *Zechariah* chapters i–viii of the biblical arrangement.

Temple after the Return from exile. Their prophecies make a series arranged in the same methodical way, each with an exact date and introduction.

An entirely new era is before us: the Hebrew Nation has changed into the Jewish Church. Politically subject, Israel enters upon a new existence as a religious community, with the Temple service as the centre of its life. It is the mission of Haggai to bring the authority of prophecy to support the new order of things. He stimulates the flagging zeal of the Temple builders, and makes this service the righteousness on which their prosperity is to depend. And he gives formal prophetic recognition (**iv**) to Zerubbabel, the princely leader of the returned exiles, as occupying the position from which the exile had deposed Jehoiachin. What Haggai has done Zechariah carries further. The new prophecy that has arisen Zechariah links (**i, iii**) to the prophecy of the old era, thus emphasising the continuity of the national existence by the recovered stream of prophetic revelation. While he brings word of encouragement to Zerubbabel, he further, on the authority of a prophetic vision, crowns the High Priest Joshua (**ii**), making for this new era the priestly and the regal authority equal: *he shall be a priest upon his throne : and the counsel of peace shall be between them both.* And again, what Haggai had touched in a single word Zechariah reiterates with varied modes of prophetic emphasis: that the old times of fasting and trouble are passed away, and such blessings are in store for Jerusalem as shall make the new dispensation far surpass the old (**ii, iii**).

Haggai

The book is a series of four Prophecies to the Builders of the Temple: each exactly dated.

   i. The hard times suffered by the community connected with their caring for their own houses before giving themselves to the building of the Temple. — **ii.** Depression at the sight of the restored Temple combated: the latter glory shall be greater than the former. — **iii.** An analogy: the touch of pollution defiles, the touch of holiness does not make holy: their two months' zeal has not yet brought the blessing, but it shall come. — **iv.** Zerubbabel shall be the signet of God [the position forfeited by Jehoiachin (or Jeconiah): *Jeremiah*, chapter xxii. 24–30].

Zechariah

A brief Prophetic Manifesto: putting the new prophecy in the position of the prophecy before the exile.

ii

This Sevenfold Vision is in form the most elaborate of all vision prophecies. The form consists in (1) what may be called an Enveloping Vision [of horsemen, or horses and chariots, who move to and fro in the earth (*Job*, chapter i. 7) as ministers of God's will]: this is brought into prominence at the opening and the close, but also remains throughout in the background. (2) Against this background of powers for carrying out what Jehovah ordains we have, like dissolving views, a succession of seven Emblem Visions, foreshadowing the great things God has in store for recovered Israel.

For the detailed exegesis of the prophecy, care must be taken to keep distinct the different 'angels' who appear.

(*a*) The Interpreting Angel: always denominated *the angel that talked with me.* Note that he is the speaker at the close of the vision: *And the bay went forth, and sought to go that they might walk to and fro through the earth: and he* [the Lord] *said, Get you hence, walk to and fro through the earth. So they walked to and fro through the earth. Then cried he* [the Lord] *upon me* [the Interpreting Angel] . . . *Behold, they that go toward the north country have quieted my spirit* [satisfied the Lord's vengeance: compare *Ezekiel,* chapter v. 13] *in the north country.*

(*b*) The Angel Horseman (also called, *the man . . . among the myrtle trees*), and his band of angelic horsemen, who are the ministers of the Lord's will. In the Opening of the Vision his band report to him; he passes on the report to the Lord; the Lord's answer comes to the Interpreting Angel.

(*c*) The Angel of the Mission in section 2. He is called *another angel,* and speaks to the end of the section, describing the mission on which he has been sent to comfort Jerusalem. Sometimes he uses *oratio obliqua*, at other times the actual words of Deity: the latter I indicate by double quotation marks.

(*d*) The Angel of the Lord in section 3, who presides throughout the trial of Joshua. With the usual avoidance of giving form to Deity, the vision introduces this as the nearest visible approach to Deity itself: hence he is once referred to as *The Lord*.

When once the form has been caught, the successive emblems are not difficult to interpret. An appendix describes the crowning of Joshua by Zechariah in the spirit of the revelation thus made concerning him.

Opening of the Vision. Angelic horsemen are at hand as ministers of Jehovah's will upon earth. They report the whole earth quiet. Appeal is made to the Lord to delay no longer his mercy upon Jerusalem: a favourable answer is returned. — *First Sign:* Horns symbolise the oppressors of Israel, Smiths the power that shall put them down. — *Second Sign:* A Measuring Line to measure Jerusalem: but the Angel of the Mission tells how Jerusalem shall grow beyond all measuring. — *Third Sign:* The High Priest Joshua on trial before the Court of Heaven: his adversary [*Job*, chapter i. 6] is rebuked, and Joshua clothed with rich [? priestly] apparel; a crown is added, and he is granted the [priestly] place of access. Finally he is made a sign of the 'Branch' of prophecy. [So the epilogue interprets.] — *Fourth Sign:* the Golden Candlestick, and promises to Zerubbabel that this supreme element of Temple ritual shall be completed by him. — *Fifth Sign:* Olive trees and Spouts feeding the golden candlestick interpreted of the Sons of Oil that stand by the Lord of the whole earth. [From the position of this sign following the two preceding ones the interpretation will naturally be that the eternal sources of divine inspiration are granted to High Priest and Prince: they are thus joined together by the epilogue.] — *Sixth Sign:* The Flying Roll or Curse purging wickedness out of the land. — *Seventh Sign: the Ephah and the Talent:* Measures and Weights as symbol of the traffic that is considered as the anti-devotional spirit: compare such passages as *Zechariah,* chapter xiv. 21; *Zephaniah* i. 11 (margins in both cases). These pass out of the holy land and are enthroned in Babylon as their natural home. [Beginning of the idea of Babylon as symbol for the 'world' in opposition to the 'church.'] — *Close of the Vision:* The ministering horsemen, with the addition now of chariots, carry out the divine mandates. — *Epilogue:* The Vision being over, Zechariah acts upon it in solemnly crowning the High Priest Joshua as of co-ordinate rank with the prince Zerubbabel in the new dispensation. He is proclaimed 'the Branch.'

iii

This prophecy is of the form that may be denominated the 'inquiry and response.' A deputation has raised the question whether certain fasts ordained in memory of the calamities of the siege [*Jeremiah,* chapter xli. 1–3; hi. 4, 6, 12] need be observed now that the exiles are restored. The prophet's elaborate response falls into four sections. [Note Zechariah's tendency to connect the new prophecy with the historic stream of prophecy; and compare throughout *Isaiah*, chapter lviii.]

1. The prophet emphasises the moral principle underlying the ceremonial: it is not the fasting itself which is the Divine element in such institutions. — 2. He appeals to the *former prophets* in Judah's time of prosperity: citing an oracle that exalted judgment and mercy: neglect of these was what brought the doom. — 3. He appeals to *the prophets which were in the day when the foundation of the house of the LORD of hosts was laid:* he cites five of their oracles of salvation and enlarges upon the theme. — 4. Then only does he give his own formal prophetic response to the question raised. The fasts commemorating the troublous times shall be feasts of gladness: love truth and peace. Two more oracles are added of glories to come for the people.

[NOTE. A characteristic of all this era of prophecy is multiplied repetitions of such formulæ as *The word of the LORD came to me,* etc. These are parenthetic, and must not be allowed to disturb the argument. I have distinguished by double quotation marks the actual oracles quoted from the comment.]

ANONYMOUS

The reasons for so classifying the remaining prophecies have been given in the Introduction, pages v-vii.

The King of Peace

This is in the 'doom form': a divine speech of promise and threat, interrupted at intervals by lyric passages celebrating the theme. [Compare the *Isaiah* volume, page 231.]
    1. Peace against external foes: hostile nations smitten, the king entering in peaceful triumph; he is garrison to his people, and the glorified people are the weapons of his war. — 2. Peace within: no false gods or false shepherds, but all strength and deliverance is from him; the oppression of the violent is at an end.

Page 206. *I will stir up thy sons, O Zion, against thy sons, O Greece.* Great difficulties have been felt in reference to this passage, as implying a prominence of Greece which would point to a totally different age from what the rest of the prophecy would suggest. There seems great probability that the words *against thy sons, O Greece,* are a later gloss. In particular, Professor Kirkpatrick points out how they obscure the image in the word *stir up,* which is regularly used of brandishing a weapon: he makes the passage read thus:

> *For I bend Me Judah for a bow,*
> *Lay Ephraim on it for an arrow;*
> *Wield thy sons, O Zion, for a spear,*
> *And make them as a hero's sword.*

Page 209. *Open thy doors, O Lebanon.* This is one of the lyric interruptions. It must not be understood as a poetic

description of an invader's progress, but as poetic imagery for
the idea of violence overthrown.   The *shepherds* are the *shepherds* of page 208 [*Mine anger is kindled against the shepherds,*
etc.]: there is no connection with the Shepherd prophecy that
follows.

The Withdrawal of the Divine Shepherd

This prophecy has been variously interpreted.   The key to
the exegesis seems to me this: in the command *Feed the flock of
slaughter* the expression *flock of slaughter* is proleptic.   Thus
the meaning is not that Israel is *described* as a flock of slaughter,
and the prophet commanded to feed them, which commission
he executes in what here appears as ii.   The meaning is rather
that God hereby *pronounces* Israel a flock of slaughter, which
shepherd and buyer devote to that purpose without compunction.
The prophet accepts the Divine decree with the words, *So I
fed the flock of slaughter: verily the most miserable of sheep.*
(Compare *Jeremiah* xxv. 17.)   ii is a distinct emblem.

As so understood, the whole makes a Threefold Emblem, the
emblems symbolising in different ways the Withdrawal of the
Divine Shepherd.

> i.   *The Flock of Slaughter*
> ii.   *Graciousness and Union*
> iii.   *The Foolish Shepherd*

i.   God pronounces Israel a flock for slaughter: the
Prophet accepts it as such with contemptuous pity. — ii.   The

Prophet [representing God] seeks to feed the flock of Israel with Graciousness and Union as symbols of his mode of shepherding. In vain: he breaks both these staves, and withdraws from his task, receiving for hire the price of a common slave [*Exodus* chapter xxi. 32]. — iii. The Prophet assumes the position of the worthless shepherd who neglects the sheep. He is thus a symbol of the worthless rulers to whom Israel is left now their Divine Shepherd has withdrawn.

Page 211. *And I cut off the three shepherds in one month.* In the absence of clear date marks to this prophecy it becomes impossible to suggest any satisfactory explanation for this historic allusion. — *And I took the thirty pieces of silver, and cast them unto the potter, in the house of the LORD.* Compare page 218: *The pots in the LORD'S house shall be like the bowls before the altar :* the two passages seem to suggest some receptacle for rubbish made of common potter's ware, a Temple wastepaper basket, so to speak.

Three Prophecies of the Siege

I have so classified this prophecy, although it is true that its second division contains no specific mention of the siege of Jerusalem. But this designation is justified by several considerations: (*a*) the position of **ii** between **i** and **iii**, with neither of which however it is sufficiently connected to form a unity; (*b*) the detail, *two parts therein shall be cut off and die, but the third part shall be left therein*, in comparison with the detail of

iii, *half of the city shall go forth into captivity, and the residue
. . . shall not be cut off,* neither of which expressions must be
understood literally; (*c*) by the general thought of all three,
judgment, deliverance, purification. (*d*) It is true that this section **ii** speaks of a land and not a city; but the association of
Judah with Jerusalem in the references to the siege is a distinc-
tive mark of **i** and **iii**.

   i.   The Fountain for the House of David
   ii.   The Smiting of the Shepherd and the Scattering of the Sheep
  iii.   The Judgment and the Age of Holiness

     i. Wonderful deliverance of Judah and Jerusalem from
the foe: effect in a penitential return to the Lord, and a
wonderful spiritual deliverance, extending as a climax even
to the false prophets. — **ii.** Judgment on the Shepherd :
the sheep are scattered, the remnant purified. — **iii.** Once
more, judgment of the siege, deliverance and restoration to
holiness.

    Pages 216-7. *The mount of Olives shall cleave in the midst
thereof,* etc. The idea seems to be a deliverance recalling the
marvels of past deliverances : the cleaving of the Mt. of Olives
to afford escape in the last extremity is like the dividing of the
Red Sea under the Egyptian pursuit; so the expressions *not
day, and not night ; at evening time there shall be light ; one day
which is known unto the LORD,* recall the staying of the sun
and moon for Joshua.

My Messenger (*or* Malachi)

The historical situation reflected in this prophecy is a further development of what has been seen in the prophecies of Haggai and Zechariah. The exile is too much a thing of the past to leave any traces. The expression of the national life in religious ritual has become so far a matter of course as to be in danger of formality and laxity. In place of this, the source of religious inspiration has come to be the thought of 'the Messenger of the Lord,' and the expectation of his advent as a power for judgment. Faith even in this is through delay losing its power. The prophecy is a call for social and religious purification, and a pledge that this Messenger of the Lord shall surely come.

Malachi is cast in a dialectic form almost peculiar to itself: brief discourses on texts which appear as interruptions from a supposed adversary, and which therefore come not at the beginning but in the course of the argument. [The interrupting words I distinguish by italics.] The whole falls into the usual seven sections: six of these discourses with interrogatory texts and a conclusion. The conclusion and the middle section are prophetic pledges of the Messenger to come.

1. A message to God's chosen people. They doubt his love: what better proof could he give than his original choice of them? — 2. A message to priests. These, who should be the Lord's messengers, pollute his altar by offering contemptible gifts such as they would never present to the governor; it is the Gentiles who hold Jehovah in hon-

our. The message [*commandment*] is that God curses
their blessings [*Joel*, chapter i. 9]; and in so doing God
is keeping, not breaking, his covenant with Levi. — 3. A
message to Judah. Judah has betrayed the wife of his
youth in marrying the daughter of a strange God. [The
meaning is not that Jewish wives were divorced to make
these foreign marriages; but that marrying within the
nation was like a wife provided by God himself for each
Israelite: to marry abroad was thus a sort of adultery.]
— 4. A message to the people: they weary God with
their impatience for the judgment: the Messenger of the
Lord shall indeed come suddenly, but who may abide the
judgment he brings? — 5. A message to the whole nation:
they are robbers of their God. Let them bring the whole
tithe, and see whether this will not bring a blessing such
as they will be unable to contain. — 6. A message to the
people: they are stout murmurers against God, crying that
there is no profit in serving God, and that it is the wicked
who are happy. But a Book of Remembrance is kept, and
a day shall dawn which shall discern between the righteous
and the wicked. — 7. Conclusion. The original message
of Moses [*Deuteronomy*, chapter xviii. 15] shall be fulfilled:
Elijah the Prophet shall be sent to heal national disunion
before the great and terrible day comes.

Page 221. *For from the rising of the sun even unto the going
down of the same my name is great among the Gentiles,* etc.
Compare such passages as *Daniel*, chapter iii. 29; iv. 1-3, etc.

Page 223. *And not one hath done so who had a residue of*

the spirit. As the returned exiles are denominated 'the remnant' (*Haggai*, chapter i. 12, 14), so the spirit of the restored
religious nationality may be called 'the residue of the spirit.'

Page 226. *Then they that feared the LORD spake one with
another.* The connection is probably this: the words in quotation marks are the desponding thoughts of the righteous, which
led them to condole with one another; and the Lord hearkened
to this complaint, etc. Another interpretation makes the *speaking one with another* a protest against what has preceded; but
the first is more in accord with the general drift.

INDEX

AND

REFERENCE TABLE

REFERENCE TABLE

To connect the Numbering of the Present Edition with the Chapters and Verses of the Bible

284

Reference Table ❧

◦ Reference Table

The Modern Reader's Bible.

A Series of Books from the Sacred Scriptures, presented in Modern Literary Form,

BY

RICHARD G. MOULTON,

M.A. (Camb.), Ph.D. (Penn.),

Professor of Literature in English in the University of Chicago.

PRESS COMMENTS.

"The effect of these changes back to the original forms under which the sacred writings first appeared will be, for the vast majority of readers, a surprise and delight; they will **The Outlook, New York.** feel as if they had come upon new spiritual and intellectual treasures, and they will appreciate for the first time how much the Bible has suffered from the hands of those who have treated it without reference to its literary quality. In view of the significance and possible results of Professor Moulton's undertaking, it is not too much to pronounce it one of the most important spiritual and literary events of the times. It is part of the renaissance of Biblical study; but it may mean, and in our judgment it does mean, the renewal of a fresh and deep impression of the beauty and power of the supreme spiritual writing of the world."

"Unquestionably here is a task worth carrying out: and it is to be said at once that Dr. Moulton has carried it **Presbyterian and Reformed Review.** out with great skill and helpfulness. Both the introduction and the notes are distinct contributions to the better understanding and higher appreciation of the literary character, features. and beauties of the Biblical books treated."

THE MACMILLAN COMPANY,

66 FIFTH AVENUE, NEW YORK.

The order in which it is proposed to issue the volumes
is as follows:

WISDOM SERIES

IN FOUR VOLUMES

THE PROVERBS

A Miscellany of Sayings and Poems embodying Isolated Observations of Life. *Ready*

ECCLESIASTICUS

A Miscellany including longer compositions, still embodying
only Isolated Observations of Life. *Ready*

ECCLESIASTES — WISDOM OF SOLOMON

Each is a Series of Connected Writings embodying, from different standpoints, a Solution of the Whole Mystery of Life.
Ready

THE BOOK OF JOB

A Dramatic Poem in which are embodied Varying Solutions of
the Mystery of Life. *Ready*

DEUTERONOMY

The Orations and Songs of Moses, constituting his Farewell to
the People of Israel. *Ready*

BIBLICAL IDYLS

The Lyric Idyl of Solomon's Song, and the Epic Idyls of Ruth,
Esther, and Tobit. *Ready*

HISTORY SERIES

IN FIVE VOLUMES

GENESIS

Bible History, Part I: Formation of the Chosen Nation. *Ready*

THE EXODUS

Bible History, Part II : Migration of the Chosen Nation to the Land of Promise. — Book of Exodus, with Leviticus and Numbers. *Ready*

THE JUDGES

Bible History, Part III : The Chosen Nation in its Efforts towards Secular Government. — Books of Joshua, Judges, I Samuel. *Ready*

THE KINGS

Bible History, Part IV : The Chosen Nation under a Secular Government side by side with a Theocracy. — Books of II Samuel, I and II Kings. *Ready*

THE CHRONICLES

Ecclesiastical History of the Chosen Nation. — Books of Chronicles, Ezra, Nehemiah. *Ready*

PROPHECY SERIES

IN FOUR VOLUMES

ISAIAH, *Ready*	**JEREMIAH,** *Ready*
EZEKIEL	**THE MINOR PROPHETS**

Announcements as to further issues will be made from time to time. Send fifty cents for a copy of any volume now ready, and give it a careful examination. Its convenient size and exceptionally attractive form will lead you to subscribe for the entire series.

These little volumes are of special value in connection with Sunday School work, and members of the different Societies, such as the Epworth League, which give special attention to the study of the Bible, find them exceedingly useful. To members of the Chautauqua Circles who read Professor Moulton's " Literary Study of the Bible " they are of special interest.

Copies are for sale at all of the denominational bookstores, or may be ordered from the publishers.

THE MODERN READER'S BIBLE.

EDITED BY

DR. RICHARD G. MOULTON,.

University of Chicago.

Single volumes, cloth, 50 cents each.

Rev. Dr. LYMAN ABBOTT, Editor-in-Chief of the OUTLOOK, writes: —

" I had intended to write to Professor Moulton, congratulating him on this work. It may almost be said that he has inaugurated a new epoch in Bible study. The scholars have been telling us for some years that the Bible is literature. Particular passages of beauty in it have been pointed out, and some single books, such as Job and the Song of Songs, have been put in literary form and given a literary interpretation by special writers. But Professor Moulton is the first one, so far as I know, to deal with the whole Bible as a collection of literature, to discriminate between literary study and historico-critical study, and to present the results of the former in such a form as to render them available to the ordinary English reader. The low price of the little volumes puts them within the reach of the great majority of American households, and I look for a large increase of interest in the Bible, for a much better understanding of its general spirit and teaching, and especially for an increased appreciation of its inspirational power, from the publication of the Modern Reader's Bible."

4

THE MODERN READER'S BIBLE

The world has waited over long for this treatment of the Scriptures. . . . The books gathered into the Old Testament constitute
by far the most important part of the Bible (from a
Godey's literary point of view), and they make up a body of
Magazine. work whose breadth and depth and height are hardly
rivalled, certainly not surpassed, in the whole world-
literature. . . . The purpose of Dr. Moulton's series is just this
exposition of the strictly literary value of the Scriptures. . . . His
book has the definite aim of supplying what the common editions
of the Bible do not furnish.

THE WISDOM SERIES

This first volume is ample evidence that the whole series will
prove of capital importance. Professor Moul-
The Evangelist, ton's Introduction discusses the Wisdom Litera-
New York. ture, the principles underlying it, the progress of
thought found in the four works, Proverbs, Ecclesiasticus, Ecclesiastes, and Wisdom of Solomon, which will form
the first series of the Modern Reader's Bible, and then proceeds to
an admirable introductory study of the first of the series.

"The Wisdom Series" does not treat the points of the text
critically, but in a literary way, to bring out the
Methodist Maga- larger and deeper meanings. They are printed
zine and Review. so as to show the poetical forms that are more
characteristic of modern poetry.

PROVERBS

New York A suggestive and valuable arrangement of the
Observer. Book of Proverbs. . . . As the Proverbs have
looked out upon us from these pages, they have
seemed to take on new force and point.

ECCLESIASTICUS

The student of the Bible will take great pleasure in the study of this little volume, and it will reward him richly.

The Christian Advocate. ... The book deals principally with the applications of ethical ideas to conduct. There is an essay on duties to parents, others on duties to the poor, and one on the general duties of a householder, including observances of religion, charity, and social intercourse.

ECCLESIASTES AND THE WISDOM OF SOLOMON

This suggestive little book cannot be perused without interest and profit. As an appreciation of the two writings with which it deals, it is simply admirable; the aim of the editor ...

The Presbyterian Review. has been rarely well achieved. By all means let this little book be read, and also the companion volumes. The " History " and " Prophecy " series will be greeted with a special welcome by many. It may be added that these brief manuals, besides being exceedingly tasteful in appearance, are very convenient in size, and are supplied with ample indices.

DEUTERONOMY

His Introduction is an explanation and appreciation, not a criticism; and certainly no one, after reading it, can

The Congregationalist, Boston. fail to share the editor's enthusiasm for the high literary quality of these farewell orations of Moses. The usefulness and value of this series is well shown in the skilful editing and helpful presentation of this particular book.

6

THE BOOK OF JOB

The Watchman, Boston.

" The Introductory Essay is delightfully illuminating and sugges. tive, and the notes are sagacious and learned. No one can fail to derive a new sense of the dignity, profundity, and symmetry of this wonderful poem from the critical treatment here applied to it."

The Congregationalist, Boston.

" It is the best edition we have seen of perhaps the greatest poem in all literature, which should be read and reread as a whole, with the editor's help and guidance. It is of the most fascinating interest."

BIBLICAL IDYLS : Song of Solomon, Ruth, the Book of Esther, and the Book of Tobit.

The World, New York.

" A marvellous effect of literary form has been produced by the recent serial edition of Biblical Idyls and Apocryphal Poems edited by PROFESSOR MOULTON, of Chicago University. One sees, as few other books have given him an opportunity to see, how much the beauty and charm of any literary work may be lost or marred by its typographical arrangement. Imagine what Tennyson or Shakespeare would be were they transposed into unlined prose, separated into arbitrary paragraphs, called verses, and numbered, and one can see how much has been lost by those who know the Bible only in the antiquated costume fashioned four centuries ago.

" Those to whom literary form makes no appeal will, of course, look upon this new departure with scant justice ; but the number of students, ever increasingly large, and of cultivated readers who will gain a new delight from this *Modern Reader's Bible* ought to make the attempt a triumphant success in many ways, both tangible and otherwise."

Additional Volume of
Modern Reader's Bible

SELECT MASTERPIECES
OF BIBLICAL LITERATURE

✠

THIS will not be a book of extracts: it will contain only complete and independent literary compositions, or integral and separable parts of the longer compositions, arranged in the form in which they have appeared in the various volumes of the Modern Reader's Bible. The selection has been made, not only on the basis of literary beauty, but also with the view of illustrating the several varieties of literary form, many of them unfamiliar, in which the books of Scripture are cast. Explanatory notes are added.

The volume is designed for the use of schools, or of reading circles desiring an introduction to the Bible on its literary side.

✠

THE MACMILLAN COMPANY
66 FIFTH AVENUE, NEW YORK

Lightning Source UK Ltd.
Milton Keynes UK
UKHW021233301118

333254UK00009B/535/P